THE VICTORIA HISTORY OF CUMBERLAND

KIRKOSWALD AND RENWICK

Richard Brockington with Sarah Rose

with contributions from Angus Winchester

VICTORIA
COUNTY
HISTORY

First published 2019

A Victoria County History publication

© The University of London, 2019

ISBN 978 1 912702 04 6

CONTENTS

LIST OF ILLUSTRATIONS

All photographs taken by Richard Pickstock, except figures 3, 6 and 20 which were taken by Ian Wells.

Maps and Tables

Maps drawn by Cath D'Alton and are ©University of London.

Table

FOREWORD

THIS IS THE FIRST FULL history of a Cumbrian parish to be published under the auspices of the Victoria County History of England, a project which began in 1899 in celebration of the Diamond Jubilee of Queen Victoria, and was rededicated in 2012 to celebrate that of her great-great-granddaughter Elizabeth II. Research on Cumberland and Westmorland was frustrated by financial difficulties and by the World Wars, and lay dormant for 70 years until its revival in 2009 (in relation to present day Cumbria) by the newly created Cumbria County History Trust, in association with Lancaster University.

Kirkoswald and Renwick is an amalgamation of three township articles researched and written by Richard Brockington, under editorial guidance by Professor Angus Winchester and Dr Sarah Rose (both of Lancaster University), between 2011 and 2016. Richard's research was strongly supported by the inhabitants of the parish and by specialist Cumbrian historians.

Kirkoswald is nine miles north east of Penrith, a remote and beautiful area between the river Eden and the Pennines, 30 miles south of the Scottish border. The church of St Oswald, for which the village is named, is dedicated to a Northumbrian royal saint, and is thought to be a pre-conquest foundation, perhaps as early as 650AD, surviving the turbulence caused by the Viking invasions to become in 1133 part of the Diocese of Carlisle. In 1523 it was made collegiate, and although that concept did not long survive the Reformation, the building known as 'The College' is now one of the finest private houses in the County, and has been the seat of the Fetherstonhaugh family for more than 400 years. Until 1603 Kirkoswald was within the English Western March, and Kirkoswald Castle was once the seat of the wealthy and militarily powerful barons Dacre of the North. Kirkoswald was a market township from 1202 and a prosperous local business and small industrial centre until 1900.

The Cumbria County History Trust, of which I am privileged to be the first chair, relies on the generous financial support of its membership and of the Cumberland and Westmorland Antiquarian and Archaeological Society, and the enthusiasm and commitment of its many volunteer local historians. Kirkoswald will be followed in due course by other Cumbrian publications, and readers who have enjoyed this scholarly and thoroughly researched book, are urged to support the wider project either by joining the Trust, or by enrolling as a volunteer, or both. In any case please do visit our website www.cumbriacountyhistory.org.uk and buy our Gazetteer (by Angus Winchester, based on the research of 100 volunteers) which contains basic facts about every parish and township in Cumbria.

Bryan Gray

Bryan Gray

November 2018

ACKNOWLEDGEMENTS

The author acknowledges the generous assistance of –

- Angus Winchester, Sarah Rose, Fiona Edmonds and James Bowen for academic support, advice and editorial supervision;
- The team at VCH Central Office at the Institute of Historical Research (University of London), and in particular Adam Chapman and Jessica Davies Porter, whose guidance has been invaluable;
- The archivists of Cumbria County Council (including Stephen White, local studies librarian), the National Archives, Essex County Council and Michael Riordan of Queen's College Oxford;
- Timothy Fetherstonhaugh and the late Margaret Fetherstonhaugh for continuous encouragement and support, their own extensive knowledge and access to their family muniments; and Canon David Fowler, vicar of Kirkoswald and Renwick (now retired), who provided many source documents used in 'Religious History';
- Michael Mullett, Jane Platt and Lydia Gray for advice on religious history; Graham Brooks for advice on industrial history and mining; Denis Irwin for advice on public houses; Jeremy Godwin for advice on palaeography; and Simon Neal for help in finding documents at the National Archives;
- Ruth Lee, who coordinated a support group of Kirkoswald residents, and contributed oral evidence taken at various times from persons, some of whom have since died. Of particular help within that group were Neville Jackson, John Haugh and Kevin Rowley, who trawled local newspapers for references, many of which have been used; Nigel Harbron, editor of the Kirkoswald community magazine 'The Raven'.
- All the many people who allowed examination of title deeds of special historic interest, and advised variously on Methodism, farming, tourism and other subjects, whose names have been given in footnotes;
- Richard Pickstock and Ian Wells, who took many of the photographs used in the illustrations, and John Jones who compiled a collection of older photographs, some of which have been used; and Eileen Brockington for support and encouragement throughout.

Richard Brockington   November 2018

Figure 1 *Kirkoswald Village Centre, as depicted by Ordnance Survey on their first edition (1860) large-scale map: note – on the south side of the Raven Beck – the College, Demesne Farm, pinfold and paper mill; on the north side, three of the five public houses (King's Head, Fetherston Arms, and George and Dragon) ringing the Market Square; and the National School (1857) in Sandhill with the Wesleyan Chapel (1821) opposite to it.*

INTRODUCTION

Kirkoswald Parish

THE CIVIL PARISH OF KIRKOSWALD lies nine miles north-east of Penrith between the river Eden in the west and the Pennine watershed in the east. It extends about five miles from north to south and seven miles from east to west. It contains the catchment of the Raven Beck which rises in the Pennines to the east of Renwick and flows west to join the Eden at Kirkoswald. The parish extends to 15,672 a. (6,343 ha.), and includes both settled land in the Eden Valley, rising from the river at 61 m. above sea level to 250 m. at the foot of the Pennine scarp, and moorland rising steeply to over 624 m. between Mount Thack Moor to the north and Hartside Height to the south. The civil parish contains the villages of Kirkoswald, a former market centre on the edge of the Eden Valley floor, and Renwick, nestling under the Pennine Edge at 213 m., as well as a scatter of hamlets (including Staffield on the north side of Kirkoswald, a former separate township) and farmsteads. Until 1700 the settlements beneath the Pennine Edge (Scarrowmanwick, Renwick, Haresceugh and Busk) were separated from the settlements around Kirkoswald and Staffield by open moorland – Whinfell, Long Moor, Middle Moor, How Moor, Scales Moor and Viol Moor, most of which had been enclosed by 1818. The parish is affected, together with most of the Cumbrian Pennine Edge, by the local meteorological phenomenon known as the Helm Wind, the only named wind in Britain which featured in geographical and historical guides from the late 18th century. A strong, cold north-easterly wind, its name reflects the distinctive cloud formation ('Helm' and 'Helm Bar'), supposedly resembling a helmet or head covering, observed to be present when the wind blows.[1]

In its modern extent, the civil parish dates from 1934 when the three civil parishes of Kirkoswald, Staffield and Renwick were combined into a single local government unit.[2] For ecclesiastical purposes, the modern civil parish is coterminous with the ancient parishes of Kirkoswald (which covered the townships of Kirkoswald and Staffield) and Renwick.

Kirkoswald takes its name from its church, which is dedicated to the Northumbrian saint, Oswald, and the Old Norse (ON) *kirkja*, in Gaelic word order, and there have been numerous variant spellings (e.g. Karcoswald 1167). From *c.*1225 Staffield is variously recorded as Stafhole, Staffull, Staffell or Staffeld, and is thought to have been a

---

1   G. Manley, 'The Helm Wind of Crossfell, 1937–1939', *Quarterly Jnl of the Royal Meteorological Soc.*, 71 (1945), 197–219; L. Veale and G. Endfield, 'The Helm Wind of Cross Fell', *Weather*, 69, 1 (2014), 3–7; L. Veale, G. Endfield and S. Naylor, 'Knowing weather in place: the Helm Wind of Cross Fell', *Jnl of Hist. Geography*, 45 (2014), 25–37.

2   Cumberland Review Order 1934.

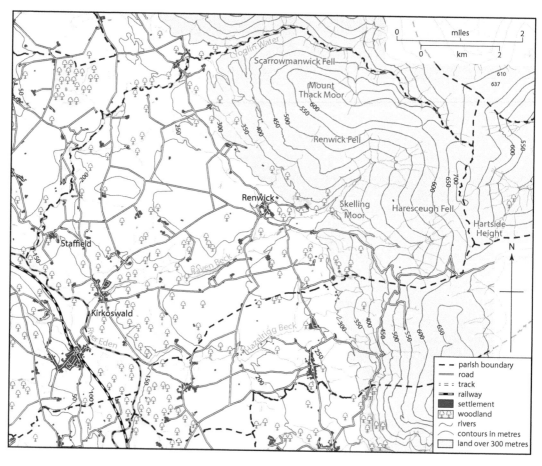

Map 1. The civil parish of Kirkoswald shown in its landscape and topographical context. The modern parish was created in 1934 and incorporates the parishes of Kirkoswald, Renwick and Staffield.

combination of ON *stafr*, a pole or post, and ON *holl*, an isolated hill. Renwick, recorded from the late 12th century to *c.*1550 as Ravenwick, derived its name from a combination of *Hrafn*, an ON personal name, and *wic*, an Old English (OE) habitational name meaning 'village or dairy farm' – possibly indicating an agricultural settlement earlier than the Scandinavian settlement of the 10th century.[3]

Kirkoswald was a significant settlement, with a pre-conquest church at least as early as 800 AD, and in 1201 an attempt seems to have been made to plant a borough, with a fortified manor house, a park and a market (Settlement and Economic History, below). For some six hundred years this was the only market east of the river Eden and west of the Pennine scarp between Brampton and Appleby, and, before the construction of Lazonby Bridge in 1762, provided a service for all communities within at least five miles to the north, east and south of Kirkoswald.

3   *PNC* 1, 215 (Kirkoswald), 236 (Renwick), 249 (Staffield).

Boundaries

The civil parish of Kirkoswald is bounded on the west by the river Eden, on the north by Croglin Water (beyond which are the ancient townships of Ainstable and Croglin, now the civil parish of Ainstable), on the east by the Pennine heights from Mount Thack Moor to Hartside Fell, and on the south by the ancient townships of Gamblesby and Glassonby (parish of Addingham).[4] The disputed boundary between Kirkoswald and Gamblesby was revised by J.J. Rawlinson, barrister-at-law, an assistant commissioner appointed by the Inclosure Commission, in 1858.[5]

From the early 18th century the township of Kirkoswald was divided for the purposes of vestry government into two quarters: in Low Quarter were the village of Kirkoswald and part of the hamlet of Highbankhill; in High Quarter were the hamlets of Parkhead, Haresceugh (a separate manor) and Busk. The township of Staffield was likewise divided: in Low Quarter were the farm called Staffield Hall (and the later mansion of that name) and the hamlet which formed the nucleus of the township, together with Westgarthhill and the other part of the hamlet of Highbankhill; in High Quarter were the hamlets of Netherharesceugh, Blunderfield, Scales, Caber and Scarrowmanwick. The township of Renwick was never divided into quarters.

Landscape

From the western boundary of the townships of Kirkoswald and Staffield, on the river Eden, 61 m. above sea level at the confluence with Croglin Water, the terrain rises in an eastward direction to 250 m. at the foot of the Pennine scarp, and thence, steeply, to 624 m. at Mount Thack Moor and Hartside Height about seven miles east of Kirkoswald. The underlying bedrock beneath the river and its adjoining floodland is Penrith sandstone, overlaid with boulder clay and sand and gravel deposits. As the ground rises to the east the bedrock changes, first to Eden shales, and then (from about 100 m. to about 250 m.) to St Bees sandstone. Further east the higher slopes of the Pennines are formed from alternating strata of carboniferous limestone, limestone grit, Alston sandstone and coal measures, with a covering of peat.[6] At the lower levels grassland and woodland predominate in an undulating landscape, divided by stone walls and outlying hamlets and farmhouses. East of Scarrowmanwick, Renwick, Haresceugh and Cannerheugh the steep slopes of the Pennines are largely bare of woodland and buildings, with the café at Hartside summit visible from afar.[7] In addition to the river Eden and Croglin Water on its western and northern boundaries, there are several minor water courses that flow from the fell-side. The largest of these is the Raven Beck, which once powered a number of mills. It marks the southern boundary of Renwick township and flows through Kirkoswald village. Townend Beck lies to the north of Kirkoswald, while Glassonby Beck is on the border with Glassonby.

---

4   QC, 5A-1a (1341, for Renwick); CAS (C), DMUS/1/12/1 (1609, for Staffield); and CAS (C), DMUS/1/6 box 8 (undated, 17th century, for Kirkoswald).
5   TNA, MAF 2/98.
6   Geol. Surv. map, 1:50,000 sheet 24, surveyed 1962–8.
7   The café was burnt down in 2017 and has not been rebuilt at the time of publication.

Figure 2 *Lazonby (Eden) Bridge, built 1762, with Kirkoswald Bell Tower beyond.*

Communications

Kirkoswald in the 21st century appears to be relatively isolated, separated from its railway station by the river Eden, and with no trunk roads (or roads which were once turnpiked) nearer than seven miles from the centre of the village. It may not always, in relative terms, have been isolated, there being evidence of earlier road systems and bridges which would once have been, comparatively, generous provision.

Roads and Bridges

From Penrith to the south-west, Kirkoswald is accessed via the village of Lazonby, on the west side of the river Eden. A bridge over the Eden at Kirkoswald was recorded in 1245/6, 1358 and 1374,[8] although its exact location is unknown, and there is no later record of it. Ferry services were recorded from 1679.[9] A new bridge across the Eden, known as Lazonby Bridge (locally Eden Bridge), was built in 1762, the year being marked on the parapet.[10] A single-track bridge, governed by traffic lights since 2014, it carries the secondary road from Lazonby, through the centre of Kirkoswald, where there is a bridge over Raven Beck (recorded in 1687),[11] and thence northwards, through Highbankhill and

---

8   TNA, CP 25/1/35/3; Graham, 'Arthuret, Kirklinton and Kirkoswald', 54; R.S. Ferguson (ed.), *Testamenta Karleolensia: The Series of Wills from the pre-Reformation Registers of the bishops of Carlisle, 1353–1386*, CWAAS Extra Ser. IX, (XXXX, 1893), 20; wills recorded in *The Register of Gilbert Welton, Bishop of Carlisle A.D. 1353–1362*, ed. R.L. Storey, 3 vols, Cant. & York Soc., 88 (1999), 231, 467, 486; *The Register of Thomas Appleby, Bishop of Carlisle A.D. 1363–1395*, ed. R.L. Storey, Cant. & York Soc., 96 (2006), 317.
9   CAS (C), DMUS/10/125; Fetherstonhaugh, A-16-10.
10   Fetherstonhaugh, A-20-46, building contract, 1760. It is also referred to as 'Eden Bridge' on OS Map 1:10560 Cumb., Sheet XL (1860 edn).
11   Denton, *Perambulation*, 57 (Denton listed bridges over Raven Beck at Renwick and Kirkoswald, but no bridges over Croglin Water); CAS (C), Q/AB/2/1, repairs to Kirkoswald bridge in 1739.

Figure 3 *High Raven Bridge, rebuilt 1781, looking towards Renwick: the road to the left goes southwards towards Appleby; the road behind the camera climbs steeply through Haresceugh to the Hartside pass, and carries the Coast to Coast cycle route; the meerstone marks the north-west corner of the manor of Haresceugh – in 1167 the western boundary of that manor followed the 'magna via de Appelby usque ad Raven', to, it is thought, an earlier bridge.*

Figure 4 *Rickergill Bridge, thought to be 12th century, after restoration in 2011 by the Office of the North Pennine Area of Outstanding Natural Beauty; the bridge carries a track from Hartside towards High Raven Bridge; Mount Thack Moor can be seen to the north-west.*

the centre and east of Staffield township to Croglin High Bridge across Croglin Water, and thence to Croglin, Castle Carrock and Brampton.[12] Minor roads lead northwards from Kirkoswald across a bridge at Potter Bank Foot (recorded in 1842)[13] to Staffield, eastwards to Renwick, and – by a separate road across the former Kirkoswald castle park – to Parkhead, and southwards to Glassonby across a bridge over Glassonby Beck, built in 1707.[14] Before 1762 the alternative route to Penrith was southwards through Little Salkeld to Langwathby Bridge, or (until it fell) a bridge built by Rowland Threlkeld in the 1520s in the vicinity of Force Mill, Great Salkeld.[15]

From Staffield, minor roads lead westwards to Nunnery and Ainstable over Croglin Low Bridge (otherwise Staffield Bridge or Nunnery Bridge, rebuilt 1701);[16] and (from junctions with the secondary road) southwards to Renwick, and northwards towards Armathwaite. Kirkoswald High Quarter and Renwick were traversed by the *magna via de Appelby*, recorded in 1167 – probably linking Brampton to Appleby through the villages along the foot of the Pennine scarp.[17] The road crossed the Raven Beck at High Raven Bridge, which was rebuilt in 1781 on the site of a bridge first recorded in 1585,[18] and in 2016 carried minor roads south towards Gamblesby, and east, via High Haresceugh, to the Hartside Pass and Alston. There is also an ancient track from Hartside towards High Raven Bridge (see Fig. 3) which crosses a bridge over the Ricker Gill (see Fig. 4), reconstructed in 2011 by the office of the North Pennines Area of Outstanding Natural Beauty.

Public Transport

Carriers are recorded from 1795 and in 1829 there were two carrying to Carlisle and Penrith and one to Alston.[19] There was a horse-drawn omnibus from Kirkoswald to the railway station at Plumpton on the west coast main line in 1866, and a railway station – originally called Lazonby, but from 1895 Lazonby and Kirkoswald – was opened by the Midland Railway on the Settle–Carlisle line in 1875.[20] Motor-bus services were established by Henry Lace of Kirkoswald to Carlisle in 1928, and Penrith in 1929:[21] they were purchased by Ribble Motor Services in 1932, and from them by Stagecoach in 1987 – in which year the Kirkoswald village bus depot, in the Lace motor garage, was closed.[22] Between about 1935 and 1975 there was a bus service between Penrith and Carlisle which included Staffield, started by Edward Lancelot Proud of Ainstable and acquired by

---

12   CAS (C), Q/6/1, 325, order for repair of Croglin bridge in 1703.
13   CAS (C), DRC 8/120, Tithe Map 1842.
14   CAS (C), Q/6/1, 477, order dated Apr. 1707 for the construction of a bridge over the 'little rivolet called Daleraughen in the road leading from Kirkoswald to Penrith'.
15   CAS (C), DCHA/11/4/6, 709, Machell's copy of Revd Singleton's history of Melmerby.
16   CAS (C), Q/6/1, 177, order to replace a wooden bridge with a stone bridge, 1701.
17   *Lanercost Cart.*, 87, item 34.
18   *Cal. Bord. Pap.*, I, item 309; Denton *Perambulation*, 57; CAS (C), Q/AB/4.
19   Baptism 1795; *Parson & White Dir. C&W* (1829), 492.
20   Fetherstonhaugh, B-17-13 & 19; N. Mussett, 'Settle–Carlisle Resources Handbook' (Kirkdale Publications, 2011) with thanks to Bryan Gray for this source; both the line and the station remain in operation in 2018.
21   *Kelly's Dir. C&W* (1929), 186; information from David Grisenthwaite who has examined Lace company records in the possession of the Lace family.
22   *Cumberland and Westmorland Herald*, 23 Jul. 1932, and 31 Oct. 1987.

Ribble in about 1938.[23] In 2016 Kirkoswald and Renwick were served by the Fellrunner bus company on Wednesdays, Thursdays and Fridays in each week to Penrith and/or Carlisle.[24]

Settlement and Population

Early Settlement

There is little doubt that settlement had existed in this area at least 1,000 years before the Romans arrived. Late Stone Age and Bronze Age monuments are found in considerable quantities along the foot of the Pennine scarp both north and south of Kirkoswald. There were in particular late Bronze Age (c.1550–1200 BC) finds of a burial mound at Old Parks Farms in 1895, a food vessel south of Croglin Water in 1961, and a burial urn in the grounds of the College in 1970.[25] Evidence of the provenance of these people is sparse, but they would have been speakers of a Celtic language, and perhaps the ancestors of the Carvetii, who had their *civitas* capital at Carlisle in Roman times. Hadrian's Wall, with its garrisons and supporting civilian settlements, lay some 14 miles (22 km) to the north of what is now Kirkoswald.[26] Assimilated to an extent while the Romans were here, the inhabitants would have been threatened by the expansion of the Northumbrian kingdom in the seventh century, and further assimilated during the period of Northumbrian hegemony to about 880 AD. St Oswald's church, dedicated to a Northumbrian royal saint, is thought to have been founded for the pre-existing community within the Northumbrian diocese of Hexham. A mid ninth-century hoard of some 700 Northumbrian stycas was buried at Kirkoswald when the kingdom collapsed.[27] In the tenth century there was Scandinavian settlement on the east side of the Eden to add to an already complex cultural mix; and some English settlement during the period of Anglo-Norman assertion of control from 1092 would also have been likely.[28] The undisturbed remains of a dispersed medieval settlement on Haresceugh Fell comprise three stone-walled enclosures, one of which has been interpreted as a house.[29]

---

23 CAS (C), DX 844; inf. Timothy Fetherstonhaugh and David Grisenthwaite.
24 Author's personal knowledge.
25 *CW1*, XIII (1895); *CW2*, LXII (1962), 27; *CW2*, LXXII (1972), 47; the author thanks Bruce Bennison for archaeological guidance.
26 A Roman water jar was found at Kirkoswald in 1894 – OS Map, 1:2500 Cumb., Sheet XL-6 (1900).
27 Below Relig. Hist.; for the coin hoard, see Lysons, *Magna Britannia*, ccviii.
28 Place-names in –*bý*, which are prevalent in this area, may be either Norse coinages of the 10th and 11th centuries, or coinages on an existing pattern following the arrival of settlers post 1092. See Gillian Fellows-Jensen, *Scandinavian Settlement Names in the North-West* (Copenhagen, 1985), 20–4.
29 NY 63250 42582; NHLE, no. 1021185, Haresceugh Fell medieval dispersed settlement 100 m. SW of Busk lime kiln (accessed 25 May 2018); http://www.pastscape.org.uk/hob.aspx?hob_id=13767 (accessed 28 Mar. 2017).

Population

Most of the County of Cumbria lay north of the realms governed by William the Conqueror and does not appear in Domesday Book. Furthermore, the period of intermittent warfare with Scotland which began in the reign of Edward I (d. 1307), and the frequent cross-border raids into Cumberland, render unsafe any attempt to precisely estimate population levels before 1600. Returns for the lay subsidy in 1339 reveal a substantial and not impecunious population. At Kirkoswald (which included Staffield) 28 taxpayers were recorded, with Margaret Dacre (who owned the manor of Kirkoswald and at least one third of the manor of Staffield) paying 20s out of a total of £4 18s. At Renwick there were 14 taxpayers paying a total of 20s 9d.[30] On the assumption that taxpaying households would be no more than one third of the total of households, this suggests more than 120 households and a population of between 500 and 600 people. The onset of plague from 1349 is likely to have reduced that figure by up to half. The 1339 figures, when compared with diocesan records 37 years earlier, and poll tax records 38 years later (both of which stress the damage done by Scots raids), suggest an ability in those troubled times to achieve rapid economic (and perhaps population) recovery in the face of repeated hostile intrusion.[31]

The following table shows the estimated population of the three townships in about 1600 (based on numbers of recorded tenements with houses);[32] in 1642 (based on the number of males over 18 recorded in the Protestation Returns);[33] in 1781 (based on Heysham's Census);[34] and the figures recorded by the censuses of 1801, 1831, 1881, 1931 (the last census in which separate figures were recorded); and the combined population for 1981 and 2001. Staffield's population, high in 1600, declined after 1700. Across all three townships, it generally increased up to 1831 (when coal mining peaked), but retracted thereafter, until the expansion of housing in Kirkoswald village after 1975 in response to the demand for homes in country villages. An influx of commuters, mainly to Penrith and Carlisle, and retired persons has filled the gaps left by a declining agricultural workforce.

---

30   TNA, E 179/90/7, rot. 6.
31   *Reg, John de Halton*, I, 195-196 (1302), and *Cal. Close* 1377–81, p. 525.
32   Calculation based on (a), Kirkoswald and Staffield, TNA, SC 11/986, survey of Crown tenements with the addition of known freehold and Alanby-owned tenements, 1606; (b), Renwick, QC 5A-23 (1603); in each case using the 4.75 multiplier suggested by Appleby in *Famine in Tudor and Stewart England* (Stanford, 1978), 199.
33   Parliamentary Archives, HL/PO/JO/10/1/82/113, using Appleby's suggested 3.75 multiplier; a single return was made for the parish of Kirkoswald which included Staffield.
34   Heysham's Census (only numbers of households, and not numbers of inhabitants, survive for Kirkoswald Low Quarter).

Table 1 *Population c.1600–2001*

	Kirkoswald	**Staffield**	**Renwick**	**Total**
*c.*1600	160	200	130	490
1642	*parish of Kirkoswald* 709		148	857
1781	560	276	189	1025
1801	634	276	201	1111
1831	768	265	375	1408
1881	595	247	258	1100
1931	466	193	174	833
1981	*whole parish*			728
2001	*whole parish*			870

The general picture is of a highly mobile population: in 1851 only half of heads of households in Renwick were born in one of the three townships, while in Staffield and Kirkoswald this proportion was even lower, at a third and a quarter, respectively. Of those born beyond a radius of 25 miles from where they lived, most (over 40) were native to Scotland, Northumberland, South Westmorland and West Cumberland. A handful of individuals came from southern English counties, and no heads of households came from Ireland or elsewhere overseas. Apart from agricultural labourers, most of those coming from southern England were either professional specialists or associated with papermaking; all but one lived in Kirkoswald township.

The Built Character

Apart from fortified buildings very little survives from the centuries before 1600, during which north Cumberland was under continuous threat of attack from the often-hostile and always-unsettled frontier with Scotland. Two-storey stone buildings in Kirkoswald and Renwick villages, in the hamlets, and dispersed farmhouses and cottages, which collectively characterise the rural built landscape, became more frequent during the 18th century. The buildings display features of vernacular architecture found widely in Cumbria, including red sandstone flagstones and ridges, stone chimney stacks, ashlar wall fabric and Westmorland green or Welsh slate roofs, which in some cases replaced earlier thatching.[35]

Settlement in Kirkoswald

Kirkoswald is recorded from 1167, although the name suggests a much earlier settlement around a pre-conquest church. The size and prosperity of the settlement no doubt

---

35   For a fuller discussion, R.W. Brunskill, *Traditional Buildings of Cumbria* (Cassell, 2002).

increased after the grant, in 1201, of a right to hold a weekly market and an annual fair on the feast day of St Oswald (5 August).[36]

Kirkoswald Castle, first referred to as a castle in 1485,[37] was the subject of a licence both to fortify and empark surrounding land in 1201,[38] and was (we may suppose) the manor house from that time to at least 1566. It was probably altered and enlarged many times, but certainly by Humphrey, 1st Baron Dacre of the North between 1473 and 1485, and by his son Thomas, 2nd Baron Dacre in about 1500 when it was moated.

Settlement at Haresceugh ('*parva Hareschou*') was recorded in 1167, Huddlesceugh in 1205 and Cannerheugh in 1345.[39] Hamlets at Highbankhill, Busk and Parkhead were also established sometime before 1568, when they feature in a survey of the Dacre estates;[40] but Parkhead is likely to be of a much earlier date, given the park was established in the 13th century.

By the mid 16th century, the village of Kirkoswald lay huddled at the foot of the hill close to the church and castle, and possessed a single corn mill. Hemmed in by the castle demesne, the College, and the extensive glebe land of the church on the south side of the Raven Beck, the village expanded northwards, uphill to Townhead. Cottages were built along the roadside at Townend before 1760, but there appears to have been no in-filling between Townend and the rest of the village until the 20th century. The area known as Quebec, on Fetherstonhaugh land between the corn mill and the Raven Beck, is thought (from its name, which appears to refer to the capture of that place in Canada in 1759) to have been developed with cottages in *c.*1760, and it is here that a poorhouse, later a common lodging house, was built.[41] Farmhouses were built on the former castle parks in 1708,[42] and between 1675 and 1720 at Todbank, Low Huddlesceugh, Swathgill and Selah; and cottages were built on Viol Moor and at Fellgate (manor of Haresceugh) between 1710 and 1760.[43] In 1781, Dr Heysham recorded eight households on Viol Moor and added 'three houses gone down & one uninhabited in the neighbourhood of Viol Moor'.[44]

During the 19th century, several more cottages were built in the area of Townhead, on both sides of the main street, in Sandhill (where also the national school was built in 1857), and beside the road to Town End (where also the new Methodist chapel was built in 1871).[45] In 1914 Sir Francis Ley, the new lord of the manors of Kirkoswald and Staffield, built three pairs of cottages for his estate workers in Ravenghyll (Kirkoswald village), near Maines Farm and near Fog Close Farm (both in Kirkoswald Low Quarter).[46] In 1925 six houses were built by Penrith Rural District Council on the east side of Sandhill, one of which was let to the police service for use as the Kirkoswald

36 *Rot. Chart.*, 89.
37 TNA, C 142/1/12, IPM of Humphrey Lord Dacre, 1485. King John visited Kirkoswald on 21 Feb. 1201 and 18 & 19 June 1212: *Rot. Lit.*, 5, 14, 20.
38 *Rot. Chart.*, 89.
39 *Lanercost Cart.*, 87, no. 34; *Reg. Wetheral*, 287–9; *PNC*, I, 215-216.
40 TNA, LR 2/213 (1568); below, Soc. Hist.
41 See also Soc. Hist.
42 Fetherstonhaugh, A-20-9.
43 CAS (C), D/AR/13; P. Hindle, *Donald's Map of Cumberland, 1774* (CWAAS, 2002).
44 Heysham's Census; below, Soc. Hist.
45 OS Map, 1:10560, Cumb sheet XL-6 (1900); below, Soc. Hist., Relig. Hist.
46 All are marked with identical 1914 datestones; below, Soc. Hist.

police house (replaced in 1960 by a new police house on the west side of Sandhill).[47] In the 1930s two pairs of semi-detached council houses were built at Highbankhill on the left-hand side of the secondary road to Croglin. In 1952 eight pairs of semi-detached council houses were built on the right-hand side of the road from Kirkoswald to Staffield, on land adjoining the north side of the Methodist church; and in 1956 another pair at Highbankhill on the right hand side of the road to Croglin.[48] In 1965 four semi-detached and one detached bungalows for elderly people were built at Croft Place overlooking the cricket and football ground.[49] Between 1974 and 2000 48 houses and bungalows (Little Sandhill and Eden Park) were built on the south side of Sandhill and Sandhill Top; and between 1988 and 1990 19 houses and flats were built in Ravenghyll on the site of the former reading room (using surviving masonry) and adjoining land, together with a doctors' surgery.[50]

In contrast to the growth of Kirkoswald village, the hamlet of High Haresceugh declined (only Haresceugh Castle Farm remained occupied in 2016), and on Viol Moor a single house still stands. Some infilling and barn conversion increased the size of Parkhead, 14 houses being occupied in 2016.

Figure 5 *Kirkoswald High Street looking southwards from the Crown Inn; on the left are Wordsley House, the Bank, 'Manor House' and Anne Dale; on the right, the Mill House.*

47   Inf. Neville Jackson and John Haugh; see also Local Govt.
48   CAS (C), SRDP/1/2/20, minute 42(4) of Housing Committee, Jul. 1952; SRDP 1/2/24, minute 67(2) of Housing Committee, Nov. 1956.
49   CAS (C), SRDP/3/PLANS/4429.
50   Inf. Neville Jackson, John Haugh, Canon David Fowler and Ruth Lee.

Figure 6 *Demesne Farmhouse, Kirkoswald: the wing on the left is 18th century, that on the right early 17th century; the Crown lessee Thomas Bartram lived here with his wife Benet (1622 datestone).*

Figure 7 *Ona Ash, Highbankhill, a late 17th-century 'statesman's' house (1693 datestone).*

Figure 8 *Huddlesceugh Hall, an ancient freehold in Kirkoswald High Quarter, late 16th/early 17th century (1601 datestone, Hutton family).*

The College, Kirkoswald

The largest and oldest dwelling in Kirkoswald, listed Grade I, is the College. Founded as a college for priests by Thomas, 2nd Lord Dacre in 1523, the building incorporates a late 15th-century pele tower, which is visible from the rear but now houses three storeys rather than the original four. After its dissolution, the College was restored as a gentleman's residence by John Maye in about 1590, and extended by Timothy Fetherstonhaugh (d. 1728) in 1696, with the initials T. F. (&) B. F. (Timothy & Bridget Fetherstonhaugh) appearing over the entrance.[51] Other substantial additions to the building were made in the 19th and early 20th centuries, including a 1½ storey extension with three bays dated 1842. Built of red sandstone walls and a slate roof, there are ashlar ridge chimney stacks to front, with 19th-century candlestick chimney stacks to the rear.[52] The interior includes a wood-panelled room with carved 1630s dates, a staircase built in 1696, and a wood and plaster ceiling in the hall with heraldic devices. The exterior includes a terraced walk, walled garden separated from the College lawns by a ha-ha, and a castellated gateway.[53]

---

51 Datestone 1696; Hyde & Pevsner, *Cumbria*, 476; see Figure 17, p. 55.

52 https://www.pastscape.org.uk/hob.aspx?hob_id=12432 (accessed 17 Mar. 2017).

53 NLHE, no. 1327056, The College, Kirkoswald (accessed 25 May 2018); https://www.pastscape.org.uk/hob.aspx?hob_id=12432 (accessed 17 Mar. 2017); Hyde & Pevsner, *Cumbria*, 476.

Kirkoswald High Street

Kirkoswald High Street contains a number of vernacular buildings dating from the 17th and 18th centuries. Demesne Farmhouse, grade II* (Figure 6), was rebuilt by Thomas Bartram 1619–21 with many bays, and later enlarged with a three-storey structure at right angles to the original in the Palladian style.[54] The (so-called) Manor House, two storeys and five bays, was built on the corner of the main street and Ravenghyll in 1706; and the adjoining Anne Dale in 1713.[55] Houses were built on the south side of the square by the Fetherstonhaugh family between 1700 and 1760 together with High College which is uphill from the market place, as are the symmetrically double-fronted Eden Bank and Hill House, both built mid to late 18th century.[56]

Ona Ash, Highbankhill and Kirkoswald High Quarter

Ona Ash (grade II*) (Figure 7), the most significant vernacular building in Kirkoswald with the only surviving thatched roof, is a late 17th-century statesman's farmhouse. Single storey when first built in 1693 it was raised to two storeys in the 18th century. The walls are constructed from square red sandstone and the roof retains a pair of upper cruck trusses. Above the door is a datestone inscribed 'W. m. L. 1693'.[57]

Huddlesceugh Hall (Figure 8) is a farmhouse, two storeys and numerous bays, dating from the early to mid 16th century, with later additions: the ground floor entrance has a Tudor arched doorway, and a datestone 'WDH 1601' (William and Dorothy Hutton) marks one of several phases of extension.[58] Fog Close and Mains farmhouses were built on disparked land for the earl of Sussex in 1708;[59] Buskrigg in the mid 18th century; and Low Huddlesceugh was rebuilt by Christopher Hardy in 1784.[60]

Settlement in Staffield

Settlement in Staffield has always been sparse. The hamlet of Staffield, the nucleus of settlement in the township, was first recorded in 1230, as were other scattered settlements at Westgarthhill, Crindledyke, Caber and Scarrowmanwick. Croglin Hall,

---

54 TNA, E 134/MISC/1619; date stone 1621; Hyde & Pevsner, *Cumbria*, 477; R.W. Brunskill, 'The development of the large house in the Eden Valley, 1350–1840', *CW2*, LVII (1957), 93–5; NLHE, no. 1144810, Demesne Farmhouse, Kirkoswald (accessed 25 May 2018).

55 Datestones – manor house 1706, Anne Dale 'I S 1713'; NLHE, no. 1144853, Manor House, Kirkoswald (accessed 25 May 2018); NLHE, no. 1312350, Anne Dale and Bridge Stores (accessed 25 May 2018).

56 NHLE, nos 1137423, 1, 3 and 4, The Square, Kirkoswald; 1144850, Eden Bank and Outbuilding; 1327037, High College (accessed 25 May 2018).

57 NLHE, no. 1137312, Ona Ash (accessed 25 May 2018); Hyde and Pevsner, *Cumbria*, 477; E. Mercer, *English Vernacular Houses* (RCHM) (HMSO, 1975), 31, 32, 41, 42–3, 103, 128, 145, Fig. 28 and Pl. 14 and 15; R.W. Brunskill, *Vernacular Architecture of the Lake Counties: a field handbook* (1974), 18, 53, 62, 69, 120, 130; see also, R.W. Brunskill, 'The development of the small house in the Eden Valley from 1650 to 1840', *CW2*, 53 (1953), 160–89.

58 NLHE, no. 1327023, Huddlesceugh Hall and Adjoining Barn (accessed 25 May 2018); William Hutton was knighted in 1604 (the author thanks Michael Mullett for guidance on the Hutton family).

59 NLHE, no. 1144824, Fog Close (accessed 25 May 2018); Fetherstonhaugh A-20-9; for disparking below Econ. Hist.

60 NLHE, nos 1327036, Busk Rigg and Barns Adjoining; 1137450, Low Huddlesceugh (accessed 25 May 2018); datestone 'CHM 1784'.

Figure 9 *Caber Farmhouse, Staffield, late 17th century, birthplace of Caleb Threlkeld.*

Charbuckle Haresceugh (later Netherharesceugh) and Blunderfield are also thought to have been medieval settlements, although not so recorded before the 16th century.[61] By that time farmsteads had also appeared at Fieldgarth, Crossfield, Highbankhill, Scales, Lincobottom and Davygill, all recorded as settled before 1568, and Raygarthfield had appeared by 1636.[62] Slack and Hill End (Caber) and Moss Flatt (near Scarrowmanwick) had appeared by 1700;[63] and new farmsteads, Burnt (or Brunt) House, Prospect Hill and Springfield, were built in Staffield Low Quarter in the late 18th and early 19th century.[64]

Staffield Hall, so called, was first recorded in 1775,[65] the name having been conferred on an ancient customary farmstead at some earlier date. A new mansion of the same name and with its own park was built in 1848.[66] Croglin Low Hall and its byre (grade II*) was formerly a tower house and hall dating from the 15th and 16th centuries

61 *PNC*, I, 216, 249; see *Reg. Wetheral* for Crindledyke p. 1252, Westgarthhill p. 1231, Scarrowmanwick p. 1260, Caber p. 283–5.

62 TNA, LR 2/213 (1568 survey): in some cases the place names are not therein stated, but comparison with TNA, SC 11/986 confirms settlement by 1568.

63 For Slack CAS (C), PROB/1615/INVX66, inventory of Rowland Brown, 1615; for Hill End manor court roll 1636 (call roll of freeholders); for Moss Flatt CAS (C), PROB/1675/WNINVX6, will of Thomas Brown, 1675.

64 Census, 1841: household nos. 5, 7, 17; Prospect Hill may have been a renaming of an ancient customary tenement called Lonnen House; below, Landownership and Econ. Hist.

65 Fetherstonhaugh, A-20-52, a tithe document of 12 May 1775.

66 Hyde and Pevsner, *Cumbria*, 478; datestone 1848.

respectively with early 17th-century extensions.[67] There were further extensions and alterations in the late 18th century. There is also an archway and gatehouse.[68] A complex building, it is mainly two storeys high with many bays and was home to the Towry family who were assessed for seven hearths in 1662, the largest number in the township.[69] Netherharesceugh farmhouse (grade II*) has a *c.*1650 wing which is two storeys high and five bays wide, and is adjoined to a three-storey, five-bay wing built in 1701 by Edmund Bird.[70] In 1723 and 1726 the house comprised of 'kitchen, pantry, parlour, white room & hair loft, dairy, new parlour, dining room, garrets, cellars, kitchen chamber, bakehouse' and 'brewhouse, peathouse loft and barkhouse'.[71] Blunderfield, Scales Fold, Fieldgarth, Park View, Sickergill, Westgarthhill, Scarrowmanwick and Caber are all mid-to-late 17th century farmhouses with 18th-century extensions.[72]

Settlement in Renwick

Before 1400 settlement in Renwick was mostly in the village of Ravenwick, with some also at Scalehouses,[73] and at a hamlet called 'Applebystreet' which lay on the banks of the Raven Beck.[74] By 1500 'Applebystreet' had been abandoned, and a settlement had been established at Outhwaite.[75] In Renwick village, by 1500, there were some 13 customary farmsteads in two rows enclosing a small green, together with a church and priesthouse at the northern end and, on the western side, a small house, probably once the manor house and possibly fortified, on what was later known as 'Castle Hill' or just 'the Hill'.[76] In Scalehouses there were five farmsteads and, by 1587, a separate freehold house called 'Slotingsteads'.[77] In Outhwaite there were, by 1550 if not earlier, four customary farmsteads.[78] Several isolated farmhouses were built in the 18th century, including Dyrah, in 2016 a ruin, which lies between Renwick and Scalehouses.[79]

Very little survives of late medieval buildings in Renwick. Across the township at large, rebuilding in stone seems to have begun after 1660 and to have proceeded slowly

67 NLHE, no. 1327062, Croglin Low Hall (accessed 25 May 2018).
68 NLHE, nos 1144823, Gatehouse to east of Croglin Low Hall; 1137449, archway and adjoining wall, to east of Croglin Low Hall (accessed 25 May 2018).
69 TNA, E 179/367/2 (Hearth Tax return 1662); Hyde and Pevsner, *Cumbria*, 305.
70 NLHE, no. 1312296, Nether Haresceugh (accessed 25 May 2018).
71 CAS (C), PROB 1723/WINVX/12 and 1726 WINVX/19, inventories of Edmund and Mary Bird.
72 NLHE, nos 1137433, Blunderfield Farmhouse and Barn; 1312298, Scale Fold and adjoining byre; 1327061, Fieldgarth; 1144822, Park View; 1137467, Sickergill and adjoining barn; 1144828, Westgarth hill and adjoining barn; 1327025, Scarrowmanwick and adjoining barn (all accessed 25 May 2018); datestones – Scales Fold 1729, Fieldgarth 1722 (on barn); Caber farmhouse.
73 *PNC*, I, 236 which refers to Ravenwickscales, thought to be an earlier form of 'Scalehouses'.
74 QC, 5A-1a, the only surviving mention of this hamlet: there are traces of a possible river crossing and house footings some 450 yards west of High Raven Bridge, identified and recorded in 1984 by Alan Richardson in his article 'An Old Road in the Eden Valley', *CW2* (1984), LXXXIV at p. 82.
75 Rental evidence from the Long Rolls of Queen's College Oxford.
76 QC, 5A-2a, 1506 rental; *Priory of Hexham*, II, 12.
77 QC, 5A-5a.
78 QC, 5A-23, call roll listing Outhwaite tenants.
79 The name Dyrah is thought to mean 'deer hedge', perhaps indicating the sometime existence of a park or hunting reserve; *PNC*, I, 236; and C. Phythian-Adams, *Land of the Cumbrians: a study in British provincial origins, A.D. 400–1120* (Aldershot, 1996, 37–8).

through the 18th century. Townhead farmhouse retains internal evidence of cruck frames, and appears to have been rebuilt between 1660 and 1700; and the adjacent Thackmoor House, much altered later, also has internal evidence of rebuilding *c.*1700. Ravenwood farmhouse, enlarged in the mid 19th century and occupying an elevated position at the east end of the village, became the seat of the squires of Renwick from 1875 (below, Social History).

A three-story mansion called Hetherington's was built on what is thought to have been the site of the medieval manor house in *c.*1750 and subdivided into five (later three) dwellings after 1812,[80] at which time – a period of intensified coal mining and rising population – many cottages were built in the village and at Spa Lane and Kilnbank on its south side, together with a three-storey house called Highland Hall (1829).[81] Shops and public houses were built in the 1820s and 1830s on land enclosed from the village green along the west side of the road constructed through the village in 1818, all of which have at various times become private houses. In 1948 two pairs of council houses were built on the southern side of the village, and there has been further infilling and barn conversion (both in Renwick and Scalehouses), but overall the footprint of Renwick village has remained little changed in 500 years. At Scalehouses, two cottages were built on the waste to the east of the hamlet in 1789.[82]

---

80   QC, 5A-191 (1827) for name Hetherington's.
81   Datestone 1829 and QC Renwick court book.
82   Datestone 1789 and QC Renwick court book.

LANDOWNERSHIP

THE MANOR OF KIRKOSWALD and part of the manor of Staffield descended through some of the region's leading baronial families, including the Morvilles and, from 1329, the Dacres. Known as Dacres of the North from 1473, the Dacres were the dominant landowners in these manors for two centuries, and they were responsible for the enlargement and fortification of Kirkoswald Castle and the foundation of the College. Eighty years of Crown ownership followed the attainder of Leonard Dacre in 1570, until the manors of Staffield and Kirkoswald were awarded to the Dacres of the South in 1649 and 1652, respectively. Manorial lordship changed hands on two further occasions thereafter: by sale to the Musgraves in 1716 and to the Leys in 1913. By contrast the ownership of the manor of Renwick has remained unchanged since it was given to Queen's College Oxford in 1341. There were several large freehold estates within Kirkoswald and Staffield, including the College, which has been in the possession of the Fetherstonhaugh family since 1611.

Kirkoswald and Staffield Manors: the Dacre Descent

An outlying member of the barony of Burgh by Sands, Kirkoswald was granted by Ranulf le Meschin, 3rd earl of Chester (d. 1129) to his brother-in-law Robert de Trivers, from whom it descended to a daughter Ibria, wife of Radulf Engain.[1] Their daughter and heiress, Ada Engain, married Simon de Morville (d. 1167), who was in possession of Kirkoswald by 1158.[2] Simon's son, Hugh de Morville, held both Kirkoswald and a third share of Staffield in the reign of King John. Evidence for the early lordship of Staffield is meagre, but Denton claimed that it was once held by the de Staffoll family before being divided, probably before 1200, between three heiresses.[3]

After the death of Hugh de Morville in 1202, his lands were divided between his two daughters: Ada, who married Thomas de Multon, and Joanna, who married Richard de Gernon.[4] Joanna and her husband were awarded her father's share of Staffield, in addition to half of Kirkoswald (the Gernon Moiety). After Joanna's death in 1247, the Gernon moiety descended to her elder daughter Helewisa, wife of Richard de Vernun; and then, in 1269, to her younger daughter Ada, wife of Ranulf de Levington; and, in

1   *Book of Fees*, I, 198; see also R. Sharpe, *Norman Rule in Cumbria 1092–1136* (CWAAS Tract Series XXI, 2006), 47; T.H.B. Graham, 'Extinct Cumberland castles', *CW2*, XII (1912), 164–7; *Reg. Wetheral*, 186–93, 287.
2   *VCH Cumb.*, I, 339.
3   *Denton's History*, 158. The division into three is confirmed by surveys and rental evidence (see below, Staffield, the Alanby/Fletcher-Vane Descent).
4   Graham, 'Arthuret, Kirklinton and Kirkoswald', 52.

1271, to Ada's daughter, Helewisa, widow of Eustace de Balliol.[5] When Helewisa de Balliol died without issue in 1272 the Gernon moiety was reunited with the Multon moiety in the hands of her distant kinsman Thomas Multon of Gilsland.[6] In 1279×83, he enfeoffed his son Thomas and the latter's wife Isabel with the whole manor of Kirkoswald and his share of Staffield, together with the park and the advowson of the church, held by the king in chief as part of the barony of Burgh by Sands, rendering 13s. 4d. cornage yearly.[7] Isabel de Multon, whose second husband was John de Castre, died in 1329, and her lands descended to her daughter Margaret, wife of Ranulph de Dacre.[8]

In 1434 Thomas, Lord Dacre of Gilsland purchased from Ralph of Kyrkeby a second share of the manor of 'Staffull' with all rents and services of free tenants, to be held of the chief lord of the fee (unnamed) – wording which places them at the level of mesne lords.[9] However, it would appear that the Lords Dacre, now holding two third shares of Staffield, became *de facto* chief lords of that manor after 1434, if not earlier, and that Kirkoswald and their portions of Staffield were held by the Dacres direct from the Crown until 1570. Sir Ranulph Dacre and his brother Humphrey fought on the Lancastrian side at Towton in 1461: Ranulph was killed and Humphrey attainted. Kirkoswald was awarded, with the baronies of Burgh and Gilsland, to a niece Joan Fenys, but restored in 1473 by an Act of Parliament to Humphrey Dacre, now first Baron Dacre of the North.[10] At some unknown date the manor of Kirkoswald was removed from the barony of Burgh and regrouped, for the purpose of holding courts, with Staffield and other Dacre manors including Lazonby and Glassonby.[11]

After the death in childhood of George, 5th Baron Dacre, in May 1569, this group of manors came to his uncle Leonard Dacre, and were forfeit to the Crown by his attainder in 1570.[12] The manor of Kirkoswald was leased to Lord Henry Scrope in 1574, and (without the castle parks) to Thomas Bartram in 1606.[13] In 1649 Staffield, and in 1652 Kirkoswald, were awarded by the Court of Exchequer to Francis Lennard, Lord Dacre of the South, a descendant of Joan (Dacre) Fenys who had briefly held them more than 160 years earlier.[14] Lennard's claim, upheld by the court, was that the death of Ranulph Dacre in 1634 had extinguished the male line of the Dacres of the North and, as 'right heirs', the Dacres of the South were entitled to restoration of the manors confiscated in 1570. Francis Lennard and his son Thomas (earl of Sussex from 1674) held the manors until the earl's death in 1715 after which they were sold to Sir Christopher Musgrave of Edenhall.[15] They descended with Edenhall until the Musgraves sold them in 1913 to Sir

5   TNA, C 132/38/11; 39/5; 39/11, IPMs of Helewisa de Vernune, Ada de Furnivall, Thomas de Multon.
6   TNA, C 132/42/4, IPM of Helewisa de Levynton, 1272.
7   TNA, C 133/73/1, IPM of Thomas de Multon, 1294.
8   TNA, C 135/15/18, IPM of Isabel de Castre, 1329; *Cal. Fine* 1327–37, 164.
9   Arundel, CW234.
10   TNA, SC 2/29/144.
11   Arundel, M517, court roll Jan. 1569.
12   TNA, E 178/576 (1572).
13   *Cal. Pat.*, Eliz. I, vol. 6, 16 Jul. 1574; TNA, SC 11/986 (1606); for the castle parks, below, Econ. Hist.
14   TNA, E 159/488. See also R.A.A. Brockington, 'Francis Lennard's claim to Kirkoswald', *CW3*, X (2010), 163f.
15   CAS (C), DMUS/2, box 26, deed 19 Jan. 1716.

Francis Ley, whose great-granddaughters, Bridget Boissier, Annabel Stapleton and Lady Caroline Lonsdale, were joint lords of these manors in 2016.[16]

Staffield: the Alanby/Fletcher-Vane Descent

A third share of Staffield, held by John Alanby in 1568 and 1606,[17] was sold to the Fletchers of Hutton in around 1607 or soon afterwards. Although this sale is unrecorded, it may have coincided with the Fletcher purchase of the manor of Skelton from Alanby in 1607. The Fletchers (later Fletcher-Vanes) were first recorded in Staffield freehold call rolls in 1639. In 1702 they claimed to own one third of the manor, and held courts from 1712.[18] When improvements from the waste were made in the 1740s the new rents were divided two thirds to Musgrave, one third to Fletcher.[19] However their claim to manorial lordship was, in effect, disallowed by an arbitration in 1795 which determined that Sir Philip Musgrave was Lord of the Manor and solely entitled to the commons and waste grounds of Staffield, and the Fletcher-Vanes did not receive a share of the commons enclosed in 1816.[20] Most of the Fletcher-Vane tenants had been enfranchised by 1825.[21] This included some tenements, perhaps 200 a. (81 ha.), in respect of which the Fletchers received the whole customary rent, and a one-third share of some customary rents in Staffield High Quarter.[22]

Renwick Manor

The origins of the manor of Renwick can be traced to a grant by Henry I to Adam de Staveley, Lord of Dent and Sedbergh (Yorkshire West Riding).[23] The manor was sold by Thomas de Staveley and Margaret his wife to Michael de Harcla in 1297/8,[24] and was held by his son Sir Andrew Harcla in 1323 when he was executed for treason. In 1328/9 the manor passed, by exchange for land in Middlesex, to Robert of Eaglesfield (chaplain to Philippa of Hainault, queen of England) who used it to endow his newly founded Queen's College, Oxford, in 1341 – the last occasion on which the manor changed hands.[25] The demesne was said in 1327 to extend to 20 customary acres, and included land on the west, north and east of the village, and the mill holme – a total of about 33 a. (13.5 ha.).[26]

---

16   *Mid Cumberland & North Westmorland Herald*, 25 Jul. 1913; vesting assent 20 Dec. 1926, title deeds of the Manor House Kirkoswald (Alan Shead).
17   TNA, SC 11/986.
18   CAS (C), DVAN/1/7/5 (general demission 1712).
19   CAS (C), DVAN/1/17/1.
20   CAS (C), DX 8/1/1; DVAN/1/7/8 for the arbitration between Musgrave and Fletcher-Vane (arbitrator Alan Chambre of Lincoln's Inn).
21   CAS (C), DVAN/1/7/7 for enfranchisements in 1782, 1784 and 1824.
22   Analysis based on the 1842 Tithe Commutation Schedule compared with Fletcher rentals.
23   *Book of Fees*, I, 199; *Denton's History*, 155.
24   F. H. M. Parker, 'A Calendar of the Feet of Fines for Cumberland, from their commencement to the accession of Henry VII', *CW2*, VII (1907), p. 231 (no.159).
25   QC, 5A-1 (also refers to previous ownership of Harcla) and 5A-1a; *Cal. Pat.* 1340–1343, 171, 191, 244, license for alienation in mortmain.
26   TNA, C 145/104 (1).

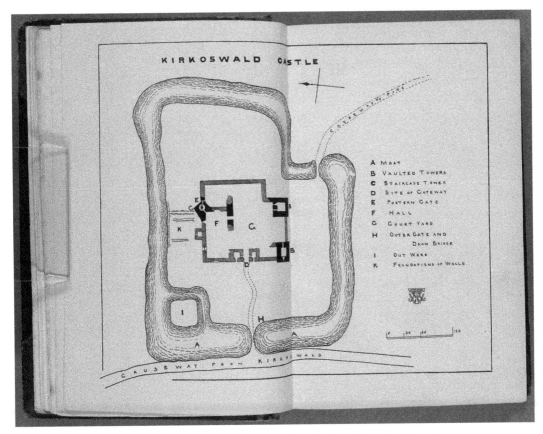

Figure 10 *Ground plan of Kirkoswald Castle, by Michael W. Taylor, CW1, II (1874–5).*

Haresceugh Manor

The manor of Little Haresceugh (later Haresceugh), which contained 386 a. (161 ha.) in Kirkoswald township, was given by Ada Engain to the newly founded Lanercost Priory in 1167.[27] After the Dissolution the manor came into the hands of Sir Thomas Dacre of Lanercost, and was held in the 1590s by his grandson Henry Dacre.[28] Between 1657 and 1671, it was sold by Sir Thomas Dacre of Lanercost to Dr Peter Barwick, physician in ordinary to the king.[29] In 1675 it was settled by Barwick on the trustees of Dean Barwick's Charity for the township of Witherslack, in whose hands it remained until 1920 when it was sold, together with Haresceugh Castle Farm (301 a., 121 ha.), to the sitting tenant Mr John Blenkinsop.[30]

27 *Lanercost Cart.*, p. 87, no. 34.
28 *Denton's History*, 15.
29 Thompson, 'Dean Barwick', 240f.
30 CAS (C), DAR/14.

Manor Houses

A manor house was in existence in Kirkoswald from an early date, for which Hugh de Morville was granted licence to fortify in 1201.[31] Though not referred to as a castle until 1485,[32] it has been categorized as an irregular Northern quadrangular castle and is made from large blocks of Penrith red sandstone.[33] Altered by various owners at various times, it was enlarged, beautified and moated by Thomas, 2nd Lord Dacre (d. 1525).[34] After the forfeiture of Kirkoswald by Leonard Dacre's attainder the castle was abandoned: the contents were removed by Lord William Howard, presumably by licence of the Crown and/or Bartram, in the years up to 1620, after which the ruins were used as a quarry.[35] Situated some 300 m. south of the Raven Beck,[36] Kirkoswald Castle was designed both as a residence and for defence – as also were the small castle at Haresceugh (of which almost nothing remains), which was doubtless the manor house of Haresceugh; and a late 15th-century pele tower alongside the Beck in Kirkoswald village, which was subsequently incorporated into the College. The building in Kirkoswald now known as the 'Manor House' is so called because it became, after 1913, the residence of the manager of the Kirkoswald estate of Sir Francis Ley.[37]

Neither Staffield nor Renwick boast any surviving record of a manor house – although it seems likely that there was, before 1341, a small fortified building on the west side of Renwick in the area now called 'Castle Hill'.

Other Estates

The College Estate, Kirkoswald and Staffield: the Fetherstonhaughs

In 1523 Thomas, 2nd Lord Dacre made Kirkoswald church collegiate with a residence for 12 secular priests ('the College'). The College was endowed with the glebe land of the church and the tithes, and upon dissolution the building and its assets were sequestrated. In 1566 they were leased by the Crown to Thomas, 4th Baron Dacre and his wife Elizabeth, but by 1584 the College was derelict.[38] Its possessions had been sold by the Crown in 1580 to Thomas Skelton, who sold them to Thomas Hammond of Essex, who in 1587 sold the derelict building with the former glebe land to John Maye and his wife Cordall, then of Rose Castle Cumberland.[39] The estate, then measuring about 70 a., was described as 'the Colledge howse of Kirkoswould or any of the other howses barnes stables edifices b[u]ildinges glebe landes and other temperall landes me[a]dowes pastures

---

31   *Rot. Chart.*, 89 (2 John, m.9).
32   TNA, C 142/1/12, IPM of Humphrey Lord Dacre 1485.
33   https://www.pastscape.org.uk/hob.aspx?hob_id=12421 (accessed 17 Mar. 2017).
34   For the park see *Cal. Inq. Misc.*, I, 439 (1291); TNA, C 135/170/6, IPM of Margaret Dacre, 1364.
35   CAS (C), DCHA/11/4/6, p. 565, Machel's (*c.*1670) copy of Edmund Sandford's memory of visiting the castle in *c.*1610.
36   NY 5595 4100.
37   Inf. Alan Shead, owner in 2016.
38   *Cal. Pat.*, Eliz. I, III, no. 2439; TNA, E 178/582: 'noe man hath taken refuge of the said Colledge nor occupied the same by the synce of this twenty yeres lasten paste'.
39   Fetherstonhaugh, A-20-1; Fetherstonhaugh, A-2-4, IPM of Henry Fetherstonhaugh, 1626; 'by fealty and in free and common socage and neither in capite nor by military service'.

fe[e]dinges closes to the said Colledge howse or Rectorie of Kirkoswould belonginge, with the tithes oblations mortuaries and profits of the Rectory'.[40] Maye restored the building as a gentleman's residence, and in 1611 sold the College and its freehold estates to Henry Fetherstonhaugh,[41] through whose family it descended regularly for 11 generations[42], except in 1797, when Charles Smalwood, nephew of the late Timothy Fetherstonhaugh, inherited and changed his name to Charles Smalwood Fetherstonhaugh. In 2016 the resident owner was Timothy Fetherstonhaugh (b. 1936). Over the centuries the College estates were enlarged with freeholds and customary land in Kirkoswald and Staffield, including John Bird's tenement (1703), the Machel freeholds (1710), Raygarthfield (late 18th century), Netherharesceugh (1821), Lowfield (1828), Westgarthhill (1860) and Dolly Tarn (Highbankhill, 1950). In 1909 the College rent roll included – in addition to farm land – a public house and 20 houses and cottages in Kirkoswald.[43] In 2016 the total area of the Fetherstonhaugh estate in Kirkoswald and Staffield was 1,112 a. (451 ha.).

Huddlesceugh Hall and the Huddlesceugh Freeholds (Kirkoswald)

The Huddlesceugh Hall estate, about 330 a. (134 ha.) between Parkhead and Haresceugh, was the largest block of freehold land in the manor of Kirkoswald. Its origins lay in a gift to Wetheral Priory in about 1205 by Ralph de Hof, and in the same year by the Priory to the wife of Robert Salkeld, subject to an annual rent of 12*d*.[44] In 1568 it was held by Anthony Hutton, gentleman, who paid a free rent of 8*s*. 5*d*.[45] The Hutton family owned it until 1667, when it was sold to William Barwis.[46] By 1675 parts of the estate had been sold for, *inter alia*, a fulling mill, a corn mill and the farmstead later known as Low Huddlesceugh.[47] Between 1711 and 1725 Huddlesceugh Hall was owned by Joseph Read, paying a free rent of 6*s*. 1*d*., and there were five other Huddlesceugh freeholders.[48] In 1812 the Huddlesceugh and Todbank estate was owned by John Marshall of Leeds and Hallsteads, and in 1842 by his son William Marshall of Patterdale Hall, whose son John William Marshall inherited in 1872.[49] In 1902 the estate was owned by J.W. Pattinson of Whitehaven; in 1948 it was sold by Margaret Anne Peile to the sitting tenants William and Robert Earl, who sold it in 1954 to the Metcalf family of Edenhall, the owners in 2016.[50]

40 Fetherstonhaugh, A-20-1.
41 Fetherstonhaugh, A-20-3.
42 Fetherstonhaugh, father to son unless otherwise stated, Henry d. 1626, Sir Timothy (executed 1651), Thomas d. 1686, Timothy d. 1728, Heneage d. 1735, Timothy d. 1797 without male heir, Charles Smallwood d. 1839, Timothy d. 1856, Timothy d. 1908, Colonel Timothy d. 1945, Sir Timothy d. 1969, Timothy b. 1936.
43 Fetherstonhaugh, B-15-7; for John Bird's tenement Fetherstonhaugh, A-19-13; for the Machell freeholds see Fetherstonhaugh, A-22-6 and A-10.
44 *Denton's History*, 156; *Reg. Wetheral*, 287/9.
45 TNA, LR 2/213; the descent between Robert Salkeld and Anthony Hutton is unclear.
46 CAS (C), DMUS/1/6/1/3, rental of 1667.
47 CAS (C), DMUS/1/6/1/3, rental of 1675, court rolls 1686.
48 CAS (C), DMUS/1/6/1/4, rentals for 1711, 1725.
49 CAS (W), D/Lec/ATK, box 194; the author is grateful to Derek Denman for this source; also *Lancaster Gaz.*, 23 Sept. 1809 (sale of Huddlesceugh Hall, Todbankhill and Huddlesceugh Mill).
50 CAS (C), DB/74/3/2; and DMUS, box 27; inf. John Haugh.

Little Croglin, Croglin Hall and the Sharrow Bay Estates (Staffield)

Little Croglin, which included Croglin Hall[51] and (before 1225) Crindledyke, was 'anciently the Beuchamps, till K. H. 7 tyme, and then the Dacres lords paramount purchased it to their seignory'.[52] Although situated within the parish of Kirkoswald and manor of Staffield, Little Croglin was an outlying member of the manor of Croglin Magna, and the freeholders of Little Croglin paid a free rent of 8s. and suit of court to the lords of that manor.[53] The mesne lordship of the Beauchamps for Little Croglin is recorded in about 1200 when a gift of two bovates of land was made to Wetherall Priory by William de Croglyn for the soul of his lord, Roger de Beauchamp.[54] In the 1220s they gave Crindledyke to Wetheral Priory (below, *Wetheral Priory*).[55] Their title to Little Croglin descended through many generations until, in 1529 after a failure of the male succession, it was sold by Johanna Lancaster, 'daughter and heiress of Thomas Beauchamp of Croglyn' to Sir Christopher Dacre.[56] Sir Christopher died in 1540, or soon after, and Little Croglin passed (probably through William, 3rd Baron Dacre, nephew of Sir Christopher) to the 3rd Lord Dacre's youngest son Francis Dacre who held the freehold in 1589 when he mortgaged it to John Dixon.[57] Soon after this Francis Dacre went abroad and was attainted, and it seems that the mortgage was not redeemed. John Dixon bequeathed Little Croglin to his son George Dixon, who sold it to Lord William Howard of Naworth before 1616.[58] After Lord William's death, and during the interregnum, it was alienated to Thomas Spence, a London tradesman, who held it in 1656, and in about 1660 it was sold to George Towry, whose family lived at Croglin Hall until 1733.[59]

Croglin High Hall is recorded as Croglin New Hall in 1712.[60] In 1745 both Croglin Halls were owned by one Thomas Johnston; in 1816 by Christabel Burroughs of Burlingham Hall Norfolk; and in 1842 by her son-in-law Sir George Charles Hoste.[61] The extent of their land in Staffield township, all freehold, was 418 a. (167 ha.) before enclosure in 1816, and 960 a. (389 ha.) thereafter. In 1873 the Croglin Hall estate was purchased by Anthony Parkin, added later to the Sharrow Bay estates, and in 1963 sold

---

51   Hyde & Pevsner, *Cumbria*, 305.
52   *Denton's History*, 158.
53   CAS (C), DLONS/L5/2/24/1 p. 215: 1633 Court Book, Wharton manors (the author thanks Ruth Lawley for drawing attention to this and related sources).
54   *Reg. Wetheral*, 256, nos 153–4.
55   *Reg Wetheral*, 280, no. 172; other medieval references to the Beauchamps are found at *Cal. Doc. Scot.* I, 517, no. 2556 (1269), TNA, JUST 1/132 d. (an assize roll 1279), and TNA C 133/112/5 (IPM of John de Bello Campo, 1303).
56   CAS (K), WDX 884/3/2/1 (for Sir Christopher Dacre: http://www.historyofparliamentonline.org/volume/1509-1558/member/dacre-sir-christopher-1470-1540-or-later (accessed 19 Jun. 2018); L & P Henry VIII, VII, p. 248 no. 646.
57   CAS (K), WDX 884/3/2/2 (the name Dixon is variously spelt).
58   CAS (K), WDX 884/3/2/3-5.
59   CAS (K), WDX 884/3/2/6; for the Towrys see *Pedigrees Visitations*, 135; CAS (C), PR 9/2, burial register, 1733.
60   CAS (C), PROB/1717/WINV37, will of Joseph Gill, 1717.
61   CAS (C), Q/RJ/1, Tho. Jonstone of Crogling Hall returned for jury service; Q/RE/1/21; DRC 8/179; *ODNB*, s.v., Hoste, Sir George Charles (1786–1845), army officer, (accessed 1 Mar. 2017).

to the Watson family who owned Croglin Low Hall in 2016.[62] Sharrow Bay estates held in total approximately 1,500 a. (608 ha.) in Staffield.

Staffield Hall Farm and Staffield Hall

The Staffield Hall estate began as a customary tenement held from the Dacres in 1568 by Thomas Lowthing (Lowthian) with a house, outbuildings and 30 a. (16 ha.) of arable and pasture, and rights of common and pasture.[63] The Lowthians attained gentry status in the life of George Lowthian (1665–1735), a wealthy man with interests in lead mining near Dumfries, who named his customary farmstead 'Staffield Hall', worth £30 a year.[64] Staffield Hall passed through two generations to Richard Lowthian Ross esq. and from him in 1839 to Francis Aglionby of Nunnery.[65] Francis Aglionby died in 1840 without a surviving male heir, and his widow Mary Aglionby on 9 February 1848 gave Staffield Hall to her daughter Jane as part of a settlement upon her marriage to Charles Fetherstonhaugh, a younger son of the Kirkoswald family.[66] In 1848 Charles and Jane Fetherstonhaugh constructed a new mansion called Staffield Hall south-east of the farm (which was thereafter called Staffield Hall Farm), and laid out 138 a. (56 ha.) of surrounding fields as parkland.[67] Under the terms of the marriage settlement, Staffield Hall passed upon Jane's death in 1874 to her daughter Elizabeth Aglionby Aglionby, and when she died in 1885 to her son Arthur Charles Aglionby. In 1920, after an order was obtained in the Chancery Division, the whole Nunnery estate including Staffield Hall was sold to the Hon. Richard Douglas (later Sir Richard) Denman.[68] After the death of Sir Richard in 1974, the mansion was sold to developers who began the conversion of the building into apartments. This work was continued by Alan and Beverley Dawson who purchased in 1986, and sold in 2005 to Michael and Marie Lawson. In 2016 there were eight holiday apartments in the main building and a further 11 owner-occupied dwellings in the outbuildings; and all other parts of the estate remained in the hands of the Denmans.[69]

Wetheral Priory/Dean and Chapter of Carlisle Cathedral

Wetheral Priory held land in Staffield: Crindledyke farm was given by John de Bello Campo (Beauchamp) to the Priory in the 1220s, and at the Dissolution the Priory also held land at Caber (free rent 3s. 4d.) and Scarrowmanwick (free rent 2d.): in 1541 all these lands were granted by the Crown to the Dean and Chapter of Carlisle Cathedral.[70] The Dean and Chapter held Crindledyke (283 a., 110 ha., in 1854) until 1891 when it

62 CAS (C), DB/74/59/179.
63 TNA, LR 2/213.
64 Denton, *Perambulation*, 328; datestone at Staffield Hall Farm 'GLB1687' (George and Bridget Lowthian). George and Bridget Lowthian registered as papists in 1722; TNA, E 174/1/7/49.
65 CAS (C), DBS/4/3/36, an enforced sale by mortgagees.
66 CAS (C), DX 556/1.
67 Comparison of 1842 tithe commutation map with OS Map, 1:2500 Cumb., Sheet XL-5 (1900 edn); datestone 1848; *Kelly's Dir. C&W* (1938), 196.
68 Denman estate deeds (Dorothy Milner).
69 Inf. Catherine Cowburn (daughter of Sir Richard Denman), Beverley Dawson and Dorothy Milner.
70 *Reg. Wetheral*, 280, no. 172; TNA, E 322/262 (surrender of Priory 1538); E 315/376 (survey of Priory lands 1539/40); *L.&P. Hen. VIII*, xvi, pp. 418–9.

was sold to Antony Parkin.[71] The Bowman family purchased the estate in 1963 and in 2016 Maurice Bowman owned and farmed 350 a. (142 ha.) at Crindledyke.[72] The Dean and Chapter also received small free rents for land at Caber and Scarrowmanwick, extinguished in the 1930s.[73]

Miscellaneous Holdings of the Dacres (Renwick and Staffield)

In 1561 William, 3rd Baron Dacre of the North, whose grandfather had held land at Scalehouses at his death in 1485, was recorded as a freeholder in Renwick.[74] His land, about 108 a. (44.5 ha.), had probably been acquired before 1485 in pursuance of a Dacre policy of placing their retainers in manors which they did not own.[75] Perhaps for the same reason the Dacres had acquired land in the part of Staffield which they did not own: in 1594, when former Dacre possessions inherited by Lady Anne Howard, countess of Arundel were forfeit to the Crown, they included (in addition to the land at Scalehouses) 11 free rentals of land in Staffield called Knypes, ranging from 1*d*. to 3*s*. 3*d*., total 14*s*. 2*d*. Both blocks of land, in Scalehouses and Staffield, were restored to the countess in 1601.[76] She sold the former in three parcels (thereby creating three new freeholders in the manor of Renwick),[77] and the latter back to the Crown in the 1630s, whereafter it was recorded in the same way as other freeholds held from the chief lords of the manor.[78]

Ravenwood Estate, Renwick

During the agricultural depression of the 1870s and 1880s Joseph Nicholson of Ravenwood Farm Renwick (1831–95), who had inherited a fortune made by his uncle on coffee plantations in Surinam and India, purchased nine customary and freehold farm holdings and other lands, a total of 800 a. (325 ha.), and buildings in Renwick (including the patronage of the church), and in the process became acknowledged as squire.[79] The Ravenwood estate was inherited in 1895 by Nicholson's cousin William Salkeld (1866–1935), and by his great-nephew George Wilfred Armstrong (1875–1956). Armstrong became owner of the whole estate after Salkeld's death in 1935, and it was broken up after the death of Armstrong in 1956. In 1910 the combined holdings of Salkeld and Armstrong were 1,060 a. (405 ha.) in Renwick and Scalehouses.[80]

---

71 CAS (C), DCHA 7/2/1 (rental 1614); Church of England Record Centre, ECE/11/1/69; CD27096 (1963).
72 CAS (C), DB/74, box 179 (sale by Parkin to Bowman, 1963).
73 CAS (C), DMUS/12/2/2 (manor court call rolls from 1645); title deeds of Caber Slack: Hugh Holliday and Messrs Arnison, solicitors, Penrith.
74 QC, 5A-3; TNA, C 142/1/12, IPM of Humphrey Lord Dacre, 1485.
75 See *ODNB*, s.v., Dacre, Thomas, 2nd Baron Dacre of Gilsland (1467–1525), (accessed 1 Mar. 2017).
76 TNA, C 66/1570, ff.9–17.
77 QC, 5A-23; title deeds of Scalehouses End Farm (Mrs Jane Fawcett).
78 See also R.A.A. Brockington, 'The Dacre Inheritance', *CW3*, XIV (2014), 291; Knypes appears to have been Scales.
79 CAS (C), DX/1705; below, Soc. Hist.
80 CAS (C), TIR 4/78.

ECONOMIC HISTORY

FARMING, BOTH ARABLE AND pastoral, has from earliest recorded times been the basis of the local economy in Kirkoswald, Staffield and Renwick. Kirkoswald has always been the more prosperous community with a richer tenantry, small-scale urban development and more significant economy (see Population). Coal mining, started on Renwick Fell in 1631, was extended to Hartside and Scarrowmanwick Fells in the 18th century. There was quarrying, both for sandstone and limestone, in all three townships, and with it local lime-burning. Cloth making, with associated fulling at water-powered mills on the Raven Beck, was important from at least the 14th century; and, in the 18th and 19th centuries, water-power from the Raven Beck was also used in Kirkoswald for papermaking and woodworking, as well as textiles. There was a market at Kirkoswald from 1201 to *c*.1830, and, from the 17th century, a wide variety of shops, trades and inns – particularly in Kirkoswald but also in Renwick. All such central place activity underwent rapid decline in the 20th century, but in 2016 Kirkoswald still had two public houses, one grocery store/newsagent, a surgery and a motor garage among its few amenities.

Farming

The Physical Framework[1]

By the mid 16th century, about 4,100 a. (1,667 ha.) were used for arable and pasture across the three townships in total. There were 1,180 a. (478 ha.) of arable land and pasture in Kirkoswald, of which 360 a. (146 ha.) lay in the village, confined to the demesne, the glebe, and the land between the Raven Beck and the manor boundary with Staffield. On the rising ground to the east of the village lay the castle and its extensive enclosed parks, measuring about 1,600 a. (648 ha.), which were used primarily as a deer reserve and (probably) heavily wooded. Elsewhere in the township, other large areas of arable and pasture belonged to the Huddlesceugh Hall estate (200 a. out of 330 a.) and the small manor of Haresceugh which had perhaps 240 of its 386 a. (156 ha.) under cultivation, the remainder being waste with small areas of woodland adjoining the Raven Beck.[2] South of Haresceugh, the hamlets of Busk and Cannerheugh, in all about 280 a.

---

1   The following discussion draws on three surveys – TNA, LR 2/213 (1568); E 178/576 (1572); and SC 11/986 (1606) – all relating to both Kirkoswald and that part of Staffield in Dacre/Crown hands; and for Renwick the Long Rolls of The Queen's College, Oxford and QC, 5A-2a (rental 1506). All acreages are given in statute a., using a multiplier of 1.8 to translate customary acreages.

2   A calculation based on OS field sizes, excluding 1842 field names such as 'moor' and 'intack'; and fields associated with Swathgill (recorded after 1650), and Fellgate and Selah (recorded after 1700).

*Figure 11 Arbitration
map (1796), depicting
farmland, including
a common field at
Netherharescugh
Staffield
(Fetherstonhaugh A-17-
36); the arbitration
concerned the level of
entry fine owed to the
Fletcher-Vanes.*

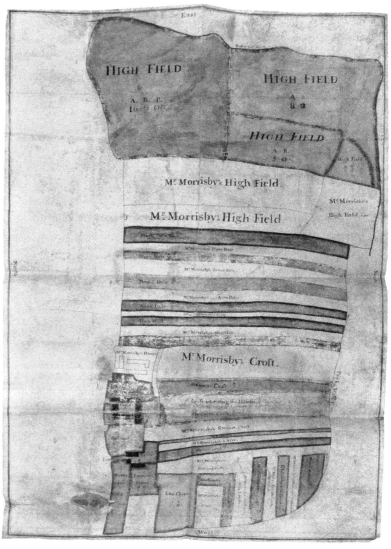

(110 ha.), were mostly under cultivation, and the hamlet of Parkhead had its own field system of about 100 a. (40 ha.).

An aerial view of Staffield in 1568 would have shown a large and irregularly shaped common, centred upon Whinfell, and surrounded by small settlements. By this date, approximately 2,000 a. (810. ha.) were under cultivation, about one third of the township's total acreage.[3] The hamlet of Staffield had around 400 a. (162 ha.), including 60 a. (24 ha.) of common known as Staffield pasture, and there were small common fields at Blunderfield and Netherharesceugh.[4] Some 17 other hamlets and farmsteads

---

3   CAS (C), Q/RE/1/21 (Staffield Enclosure Award and map).
4   For Netherharesceugh, see Fetherstonhaugh, A-17-36 (see Figure 11); for Blunderfield CAS (C), Q/RE/1/21 (enclosure map).

Figure 12 *Renwick head dyke, looking towards Outhwaite to the south east; the land on the left-hand side was assarted in the 15th century; the footpath to the right is called 'Beggars' Trod'.*

were scattered across the township, the largest being Crindledyke (240 a., 96. ha.) and Croglin Hall (346 a., 140 ha.).

Cultivated land in Renwick had until 1450 been limited to about 750 a. (309 ha.). However, by 1500 this had been increased to about 920 a. (379 ha.) by assarting land to the north and east of the village up to the 220–40 m. contour.[5] While common fields were few and small in Kirkoswald and Staffield, there were large common fields to the north, west and south of Renwick village; and two hamlets, Scalehouses north of the village, and Outhwaite east of the village, both with their own field systems.[6]

All three townships had large areas of unenclosed waste, both on the high ground (above 250 m.) to the east, and on lower ground. There were 5,591 a. (2,152 ha.) on the Pennine scarp, of which nearly half (2,525 a., 1,004 ha.) lay in Renwick; Kirkoswald had 1,950 a. (790 ha.), and Staffield 1,116 a. (448 ha.). Of the three townships, Staffield had the most unenclosed waste on the lower ground, amounting to some 2,500 a. (1,012 ha.) on Whinfell Common; in Kirkoswald there were Berrymoor Common (Highbankhill) and Viol Moor (300 a., 121 ha.); and in Renwick, Long Moor and Middle Moor (850 a., 350ha). In total, unenclosed waste amounted to about 9,241 a. (3,635 ha.). The tenantry of all three townships had common rights on their own sections of the high fellsides.[7]

5   Rental evidence (QC, Long Rolls from 1350), and traces of a medieval head dyke at about 200 m.

6   CAS (C), D/RGL/18, pre-enclosure map, 1815; C. and J. Greenwood, *Map of the County of Cumberland* (1823).

7   Fetherstonhaugh, B-17-3 (evidence given to commissioners for the 1876 enclosure).

*Map 2. Changing land use in
Kirkoswald, Renwick and Staffield.
The area which comprises the modern
civil parish of Kirkoswald showing
the location and dates of private and
parliamentary enclosure, the location of
Renwick's common fields, and ancient
parish boundaries.*

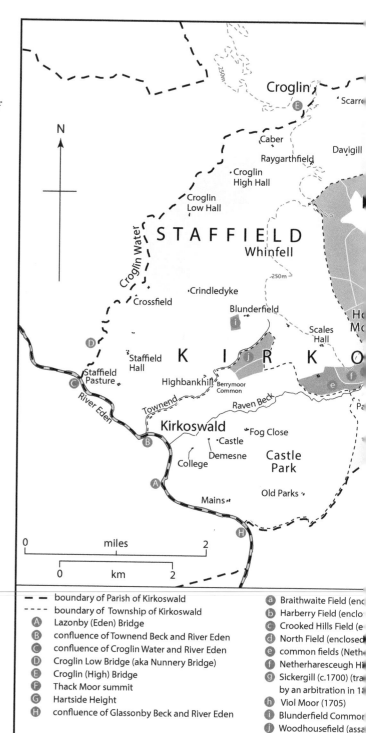

boundary of Parish of Kirkoswald
boundary of Township of Kirkoswald
Ⓐ   Lazonby (Eden) Bridge
Ⓑ   confluence of Townend Beck and River Eden
Ⓒ   confluence of Croglin Water and River Eden
Ⓓ   Croglin Low Bridge (aka Nunnery Bridge)
Ⓔ   Croglin (High) Bridge
Ⓕ   Thack Moor summit
Ⓖ   Hartside Height
Ⓗ   confluence of Glassonby Beck and River Eden

ⓐ   Braithwaite Field (enc
ⓑ   Harberry Field (enclo
ⓒ   Crooked Hills Field (e
ⓓ   North Field (enclosed
ⓔ   common fields (Neth
ⓕ   Netherharesceugh Hi
ⓖ   Sickergill (c.1700) (tra
       by an arbitration in 1
ⓗ   Viol Moor (1705)
ⓘ   Blunderfield Common
ⓙ   Woodhousefield (assa

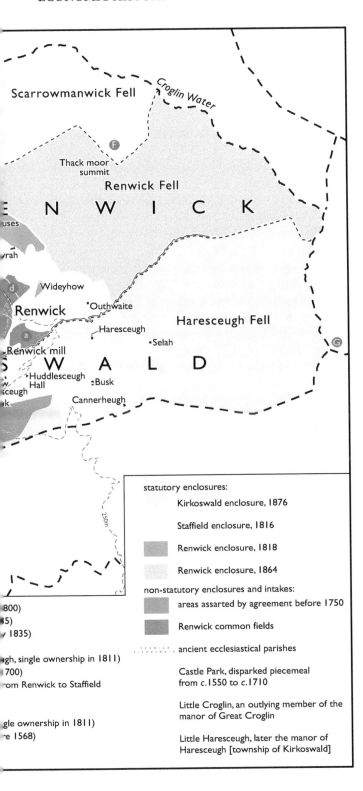

Scarrowmanwick Fell

Croglin Water

Thack moor
summit

Renwick Fell

E N W I C K

uses

rah

Wideyhow

'Outhwaite

Renwick

Haresceugh Fell

Haresceugh

•Selah

Renwick mill

S W A L D

•Huddlesceugh
Hall   :Busk

sceugh

Cannerheugh

statutory enclosures:

Kirkoswald enclosure, 1876

Staffield enclosure, 1816

Renwick enclosure, 1818

Renwick enclosure, 1864

non-statutory enclosures and intakes:

areas assarted by agreement before 1750

Renwick common fields

.... ancient ecclesiastical parishes

Castle Park, disparked piecemeal
from c.1550 to c.1710

Little Croglin, an outlying member of the
manor of Great Croglin

Little Haresceugh, later the manor of
Haresceugh [township of Kirkoswald]

800)

5)

1835)

gh, single ownership in 1811)

700)
om Renwick to Staffield

gle ownership in 1811)
e 1568)

The rights of Renwick tenants on Long and Middle Moors were subject to an agistment between 1592 and 1650.[8]

By 1568, the disparking of the Kirkoswald castle parks had begun, with some 260 a. (104 ha.) having been enclosed, including Woodhousefield, Castle Close, Sheep Close and Maynes Close.[9] In 1606, these enclosed areas were leased by the Crown to a local farmer. The remaining parks, used for grazing and pannage and kept secure by locked park gates, were leased from 1592.[10] From 1619 to 1668 Henry Fetherstonhaugh and Stephen Bowman, and their heirs, each held a moiety of the unenclosed parks.[11] Having been awarded lordship of the manor of Kirkoswald in 1652, the Lennards renewed leases of the demesne and former parkland in 1677 and 1687.[12] In 1708, reference was made to the earl of Sussex 'building farm houses in his parks'.[13] By 1712 the parkland had been fully enclosed and the gates removed, while the parks and demesnes had been divided into six farms and leased for periods of between seven and 12 years.[14]

There was also voluntary enclosure of wastes in the 17th and early 18th century. In the manor of Haresceugh, the farmstead of Swathgill was recorded in 1653, and the farmstead of Selah in 1721, probably both including intakes.[15] By 1721 all Haresceugh waste had been enclosed with the exception of an area of pasture by the Raven Beck where a system of cattlegates applied. In Renwick land at the south-west corner of the manor was intaken in the 1690s and added to lands in both Renwick and Staffield to create a new farmstead at Sickergill in about 1720.[16] In 1697 the earl of Sussex and his Kirkoswald and Staffield tenantry agreed on measures for enclosing and improving waste grounds within both manors; and an agreement was made in 1699 between Sussex and Edmund Bird to enclose 70 a. (30 ha.) of Howe Moor at High Field, Netherharesceugh, the Fletchers receiving a share.[17] By agreement, in about 1705, 178 a. (72 ha.) of Viol Moor were enclosed.[18] The Low Huddlesceugh and Todbank farmsteads (Kirkoswald) seem also to have been created before 1750, their lands being a combination of sales and lettings from the Huddlesceugh Hall estate and the Viol Moor enclosures.[19]

There was however no further enclosure by agreement in Staffield, perhaps because of the disputed claims by the Fletchers to a share of the commons.[20] Instead there was a

8   QC, 5A-9, grant of sheepwalk to William Bowman.
9   TNA, E 214/300 (1613, reciting a lease in 1592); TNA, LR 2/213.
10   TNA, SC 11/986 (1606); CAS (C), DMUS, box 26.
11   TNA, E 134/17Jas1/Mich2; CAS (C), DMUS, box 27; ERO, Barrett-Lennard D/DL C28; Fetherstonhaugh, A-20-8.
12   ERO, Barrett-Lennard D/DL M79/1; Denton, *Perambulation*, 327, gives the value of demesne and parks as £200 pa; CAS (C), DMUS, box 69.
13   Fetherstonhaugh, A-20-9.
14   ERO, Barrett-Lennard D/DL M79/1 and M79/2.
15   For Swathgill, 1653 burial, and field names, e.g. 'Intack'; for Selah (1721), see Thompson, 'Dean Barwick', 267.
16   QC, Renwick Court Book, 71, 110, 129.
17   Fetherstonhaugh, A-17-19; A-17-36 for Farthest High Field held from Fletcher.
18   CAS (C), DMUS/1/6, manor court on 27 Oct. 1709 lists free tenants for the improvement of Viol Moor.
19   CAS (C), PROB/1797/W/129, will of Christopher Hardy of Low Huddlesceugh; for Todbank, Heysham's census.
20   CAS (C), DX 8/1/1; TNA, C 8/597/55 (pleadings in Earl of Sussex *v.* Fletcher, 1704, a case which did not come to trial).

continuation of a long tradition of piecemeal intakes: four tenants had been recorded in 1568 as having added to their farmland by improving waste, three at Scarrowmanwick and one at Slobyfield (unidentified).[21] In 1636 two tenements had been recorded at Raygarthfield, with at least one farmstead built on land recently assarted from the waste south of Caber and Scarrowmanwick;[22] the Raygarthfield farmstead was purchased by the Fetherstonhaughs after 1750. By 1640 cottages and farmsteads had been built at Hill End and Slack, east of Caber farmstead and west of Lincobottom;[23] and new customary rents had been created at Sickergill in 1662.[24] In 1725 16 tenants were presented for encroachments on the common since 1676: they included the intakes at Sickergill, and Highbankhill, mentioned above; High Field at Netherharesceugh; five intakes at Scales with the removal of the ring fence and the creation of garths and two barns; two intakes on which houses were built at Hill End and Davygill; and one involving the removal of the ring hedge at Croglin Hall, where in about 1700 a second farmstead, later known as Croglin High Hall, had been built. In 1735 23 Staffield tenants were amerced for enclosing common (presumably since 1725); and one was amerced for having a malt kiln on the common. New rents for most of these were recorded in 1743 in the proportion two parts Musgrave to one part Fletcher.[25]

By 1750 the total area under cultivation and pasture had increased to about 2,800 a. (1,130 ha.) in Kirkoswald, and about 2,100 a. (850 ha.) in Staffield, but remained unchanged at 920 a. (379 ha.) in Renwick. At about that time the long process of exchanging strips and dales in the Renwick common fields began, and with it the creation of small enclosed fields. By 1800 Braithwaite Field (south of the village), and by 1812 the North Field, were completely enclosed: Harberry and Crooked Hills common fields on the west side of the village were not fully enclosed until about 1835.[26] In the meantime Acts of Parliament had been obtained, and enclosure awards made, for both Renwick and Staffield.[27] The Renwick award dealt with Long Moor and Middle Moor (and the village common and other small parcels); the Staffield award dealt with both Whinfell Common and the Pennine scarp east of Scarrowmanwick. The high fells east of Renwick were enclosed in 1864, and those east of Haresceugh and Busk (together with the rest of Viol Moor and Berrymoor Common) in 1876.[28] In 1816 Charles Smalwood Fetherstonhaugh (1762–1839) carried out extensive improvements to the east bank of the Eden, singling the course of the river and recovering for agricultural use the area known as the Willow Beds.[29]

21   TNA, LR 2/213. In all four cases rent was payable to Alanby as well as the Dacre overlords.
22   CAS (C), DMUS/1/12/1; baptism 1647 (Muncaster of Regarthfield); Fetherstonhaugh, A-2-5, 1630.
23   CAS (C), DMUS/1/12/1, court rolls from 1636, passim.
24   CAS (C), DMUS/1/12/1, manor court 20 Oct. 1662, rents payable to Lennard.
25   CAS (C), DVAN/1/17/1.
26   QC, 5A-191; date stone 1812.
27   Staffield Enclosure Act 1806; Renwick Enclosure Act 1814; CAS (C), Q/RE/1/21, Staffield Enclosure Award,1816; CAS (C), Q/RE/1/53, Renwick Enclosure Award, 1818.
28   CAS (C), SPC/35/1, Renwick, 1864; CAS (C), QRE/125, Kirkoswald, 1876.
29   Fetherstonhaugh, *Our Cumberland Village*, 71, 75, 77, transcript of an estate book now lost.

Agrarian Institutions

In Kirkoswald in 1568 land tenure was divided between freeholds and customary tenements, with leasing of the demesne and part of the parks. The largest freehold estate in 1568 was Huddlesceugh Hall, yielding a free rent of 8s. 5d.; and after 1580 the former glebe land would become freeholds of the College estate. Ancient customary tenures included Parkhead, held in two tenements, combined rent 7s. 11d.; Busk and Cannerheugh, four customary tenements, combined rent 36s. 2d.; and 14 tenements in and around the village of Kirkoswald, total rents about £3, most very small.[30] From 1619 all the Kirkoswald customary tenants east of the parks were listed as leaseholders, but after 1652 they reverted to tenant right tenure at the previous rents.[31] Parcels of Viol Moor, after enclosure in about 1705, were held freehold subject to free rents.[32] From the mid 18th century there were four farms on the former Kirkoswald parkland – Highbankhill, Fog Close, Mains, Old Parks – and all four, together with Demesne Farm, were leased, leasehold thereby becoming the dominant tenure in Kirkoswald until the farms of the former parks were sold to sitting tenants in the 1980s. In 1795 the manor of Haresceugh included demesne land and 12 customary rentals, totalling £1 12s. p.a.[33]

In Staffield, much of the old farmland was ancient freehold, the enfranchisement of which is unrecorded. In 1636 many Staffield farmers held a mixture of freeholds (either rent free or paying free rents to the Crown, the Fletchers or the Dean and Chapter of Carlisle Cathedral), and land held by custom of the manor from either the Crown, the Fletchers or the Bells.[34] Customary tenure predominated in Low Quarter: farmers in High Quarter had larger freeholds.[35] Croglin Hall and Crindledyke were freeholds held by third parties and leased or tenanted. In 1675 the earl of Sussex received annual rents of £8 9s. 5d. from 51 customary tenants, and free rents of 4s. 3d. from six freeholders; and in 1743 Henry Fletcher received annual rents of £3 4s. 5d. from 22 customary tenants, and free rents of 1s. 11d. from six freeholders (two of whom were also customary tenants). Of the Fletcher tenants, 11 appear also in Musgrave rentals, the proportion of rent in all these cases being two parts Musgrave to one part Fletcher.[36] Some 20 of the Musgrave rentals were less than one shilling and two were described as cottages: there were several other cottages within the hamlets, on small parcels of freehold land and on intakes from the waste.[37]

In Renwick in 1571 all the farmland was held by tenant right in 19 customary tenements (total rent about £7 6s.),[38] except for the former demesne and glebe land, which were freehold, and land at Scalehouses owned by the Dacres (freehold from 1603).

30   TNA, LR 2/213; by 1606 Cannerheugh was a single tenement rent 18s. 1d. and Busk 2 tenements rent 9s. 1/2d. each: TNA, SC 11/986.
31   CAS (C), DMUS/1, box 8, manor court call rolls, 1619; CAS (C), HNC/165/2, an *inspeximus* of a 1610 document which may explain the temporary change to leasehold.
32   CAS (C), CMBE/1/4/1.
33   CAS (C), D/WAL/5; D/AR/13.
34   CAS (C), DMUS/1/12/1, manorial call rolls from 1636.
35   CAS (C), Q/RJ/1.
36   CAS (C), DMUS/1/12/1; DVAN/1/7/1.
37   CAS (C), DX 8/1/1; the 1675 rental lists two cottages as recent additions.
38   QC, 5A-4 and 5A-6 refer to 'tenant right'.

Most tenements, both freehold and customary, held between 30 and 40 a. (13–17 ha.).[39] A single cottage in Renwick village was recorded in 1597.[40] It was the ancient custom in Renwick to remove all livestock from the common fields to the upland waste at mid-April day, and return them, after harvest, at Michaelmas.[41] The Renwick manor court took pains to enforce the movement of livestock, and appointed frithmen, as late as 1733; and after the enclosure of the moorland west of Renwick in 1818 a stints committee was appointed to control grazing rights on the high fells.[42]

Most Kirkoswald tenants owed boon services (days of work and loads of coal) until the Interregnum.[43] Staffield tenants also owed boon services to the chief lords, amounting to 25 days between them, although manor court rolls from 1636 make no further mention of this obligation; Fletcher rents sometimes included hens in addition to money.[44] Boon services were not recorded in Renwick. An annual payment for greenhew was recorded both in Renwick and Staffield until 1680, but never in Kirkoswald.[45] Before 1652 Kirkoswald and Staffield tenants paid an entry fine of four times the annual rent: this was raised to six times the annual rent in 1661.[46] In 1676 the tenants of both Kirkoswald and Staffield purchased the right to pay entry fines of one penny, in exchange for payment to the earl of Sussex of a lump sum of 30 times the annual rent.[47] Entry fines in Renwick were twice the annual rent until 1630 when they were raised by agreement to 12 times the annual rent, and remained unchanged thereafter.[48] The Fletchers retained the right to levy arbitrary entry fines on their Staffield tenants – at 20 times the annual rent in 1712, rising to 88 times the annual rent in 1801.[49]

In 1736 tenant right land held by the Fetherstonhaughs in Kirkoswald and Staffield was enfranchised,[50] and most Fletcher tenancies in Staffield were enfranchised between 1782 and 1824;[51] but all other customary holdings remained so until the 20th century.

Apart from the castle park farms and the Haresceugh demesne, which were subject to leases until the 20th century, most tenants farmed their own land until about 1750, but by 1842 there had been substantial underletting in all three townships, and in 1910 and 1941 leasehold and tenant farming predominated.[52] The sale, usually to sitting tenants, of the Ravenwood estates in Renwick in 1956, of the Sharrow Bay estates in Staffield in

39   Analysis from CAS (C), DRC 8/161, Renwick Tithe Commutation Award (1842) and earlier manor court rolls.
40   QC, 5A-13.
41   QC, 5A-10; see also CAS (C), DMUS/1/12/1, Netherharesceugh.
42   QC, Renwick Court Book, 234 and 5A-191, item 37 and later manor court rolls, passim.
43   CAS (C), DMUS/1, box 8, court of 9 Mar. 1630/1.
44   TNA, E 178/576; CAS (C), DVAN/1/7/1 for hens.
45   For Renwick, QC manorial call rolls passim; for Staffield, TNA, SC 2/165/22 and CAS (C), DMUS/1/12/1.
46   TNA, SC 2/165/17, memo of amercements, 1605; CAS (C), DMUS/1/6/1/3, court of 5 Sept. 1661.
47   CAS (C), DMUS/2/box 27.
48   QC, 5A-49 and 5A-56.
49   Fetherstonhaugh, A-17-20 and A-17-37, both relating to Netherharesceugh.
50   Fetherstonhaugh, A-19-29.
51   CAS (C), DVAN/1/7/7 and 1/7/8.
52   CAS (C), Tithe Schedules 1842 and TIR 4/8; TNA, MAF 32/183/159.

the 1960s, and the castle park farms in the 1980s, reasserted the dominance of owner-occupation.[53]

In 1842, all the farms on the former castle parks, and the College, Demesne, Huddlesceugh Hall, Haresceugh Castle and Cannerheugh farms, were more than 100 a. (41 ha.) in extent; and the average size of the 28 farms in Staffield was over 150 a. (61 ha.).[54] The Kirkoswald enclosure of 1876, and a reduction in numbers of farms in Staffield to 22, further increased the average size of farms, a few exceeding 500 a. (203 ha.) by 1910. By contrast, most farms in Renwick, Parkhead, Busk and Haresceugh remained small (40–100 a., 16–41 ha.) until 1945.

In 1797 a male farmhand received 1s. or 1s. 2d. plus victuals for each day at harvest; women 2d. less. In 1834 an agricultural labourer received 10s. per week, without cider or beer.[55] In 1841 in Kirkoswald there were a total of 103 men employed in agriculture, comprising 25 farmers and 78 agricultural labourers and resident farm servants; by 1901 the number had fallen to 75.[56] While the number of farmers remained buoyant (24 farmers and one market gardener), there were just 50 agricultural labourers, including 'farmers' sons', a forester and two gamekeepers, and resident farm servants. In Staffield, in 1841, 107 men (including farmers' sons aged 15 and above) were working on the land; in 1901 there were 75.[57] The 20th century saw a marked decline in agricultural employment across all three townships; in 2016, total employment on the land was about 48.[58]

Crops and Livestock Production

In Tudor and Stuart times most farmers in what would later be known as the Low Quarters of Kirkoswald and Staffield practised mixed farming with small numbers of cattle and sheep: crops were usually oats, barley and rye, but occasionally included wheat.[59] A few Low Quarter farmers had large flocks and herds – for example, William Bowman of Demesne Farm, Kirkoswald (d. 1620), who had 30 cattle and 160 sheep, contracted for the use of grazing on the parks and sought agistment in Renwick.[60] Large-scale animal husbandry, in addition to arable farming, was more common in the High Quarters of both townships. After 1660 there were several farmers in all three townships with flocks exceeding 100 sheep.[61] In Renwick, where good pasture was scarce and needed by most households for small-scale dairying and for horses,[62] the main source of

53   For Ravenwood estate sales, title deeds of Horse & Jockey Inn (Mrs A St John) and inf. Hardy Greenop; for Sharrow Bay sales CAS (C), DB/74, box 178; for Castle Park farms inf. James Raine (Fog Close Farm) and Robert Pickthall (Mains Farm) and Timothy Fetherstonhaugh.
54   CAS (C), Tithe Commutation Schedules; DMus/5/4/3, box 70, leases of the castle park farms, 1791/3; TIR 4/78 (1910).
55   Eden, *State of the Poor*, 84; *Poor Law Com. 1st Rep.*, p. 112a (image 1815).
56   Census 1841, 1901 for Kirkoswald – excludes farmers' wives and children.
57   Census 1841, 1901 for Staffield.
58   Author's head count in consultation with farmers.
59   CAS (C), PROB series, wills and inventories between 1564 and 1600.
60   QC, 5A-9 and 5A-54; TNA, SC 11/986; CAS (C), PROB/1620/WINVX18, will and inventory of William Bowman, 1620.
61   CAS (C), PROB series, wills and inventories, 1660 and 1700.
62   CAS (C), PROB/1739/AINVX5, inventory of Jonathan Barker, 1739; PROB/1742/WINV/744(a), inventory of William Watson, 1742.

income was sheep farming, from which, according to Thomas Denton, some Renwick men became 'very rich'.[63]

Late 18th-century commentators on agriculture in Kirkoswald and Staffield described the soil as loamy and some parts clay and 'very fertile in wheat, barley and oats—some of the lowlands subject to water … the east cold and mountainous—a good sheep common.' In 1794 sheep were chiefly short Scots, but cross-breeding was practised to improve the quality of wool; the highest grounds and coarsest herbage produced the heaviest sheep and coarser wool. By this time, there were several farmers with herds of 20 or more cows, including 'the long-horned sort, such as are bred in Lancashire and Westmorland.' Husbandry was of a high standard: the land was 'very productive' due to fallowing, liming and manuring, and crops of turnips, clover and hay.[64] About Renwick, where the pattern of small farms remained largely unchanged until the 20th century, it was said that the soil was 'cold and unfruitful', crops were oats barley and some potatoes, and there were some 2,000 sheep with no attention paid to improving the breed.

The Musgraves routinely included land improvement clauses in leases of the demesne and park farms after 1760.[65] In the 1850s Timothy Fetherstonhaugh (1811–56) invested in drainage by clay tiles, and in 1852 his farmland was described as 'exceedingly well managed' with 'the best and purest stock of cattle sheep and pigs'.[66] In 1897 the soil of Kirkoswald and Staffield was 'very fertile and well cultivated, generally of a light gravely nature, the bottom lands loam and clayey, and the subsoil clay and gravel', and the principal crops were turnips, potatoes, oats and barley, grown it seems for both human and livestock consumption.[67] At Cannerheugh, at the turn of the century, water power from Cannerheugh Beck was used to drive a threshing machine;[68] but by that time the corn mills at Raven Bridge, Renwick and Parkhead had all closed, leaving only the mill in Kirkoswald to provide a service until that too closed in 1953.[69]

In 1941, across the three townships, oats and potatoes were grown for human consumption, with some wheat at Lowfield and Fieldgarth (both on low-lying ground adjoining the Eden). Most farms included dairies and flocks of sheep, but only six Staffield farms (Crindledyke, Caber, Raygarthfield, Davygill and the two farms at Scarrowmanwick) and Outhwaite Farm at Renwick were large-scale sheep farms, making extensive use of grazing on the high fells.[70] The long term trend away from arable and towards animal husbandry intensified after 1945: Kirkoswald farmers were much involved in the formation of the Bluefaced Leicester Sheep Breeders Association, the first meeting of which was held at the Kirkoswald Church Institute in 1962, the first elected chairman being Joe Raine of Old Parks Farm.[71] From that time it became general practice

---

63   Denton, *Perambulation,* 330.
64   Hutchinson, *Hist. Cumb.,* I, 210, 212 (all quotations from Housman's notes).
65   CAS (C), DMUS, box 69.
66   Fetherstonhaugh, A-3-3 (1852), A-18-60 (1855); W. Dickinson, 'Farming of Cumberland', *Journal of the Royal Agricultural Society of England,* vol. 13 (1852), 224 (with thanks to Andrew Humphries for this reference).
67   *Kelly's Dir. Cumb.* (1897), 196.
68   OS Map, 1:2500 Cumb., Sheet XL-8 (1900 edn); inf. Tom Bowman and John Haugh.
69   *Penrith Observer,* 30 Jan. 1953.
70   TNA, MAF 32/183/159.
71   Jeremy Hunt, *The Bluefaced Leicester, a History of the Breed* (Penrith, 1986), 26.

to breed 'border crosses', Swaledale bred with Blue Leicester and more recently Texels. While dairying remained general (up to the 1990s), the most common breed of cattle was Friesian; but with the reduction in dairying, French breeds like Limousins became more usual.

In 2016 there were nine working farms in Kirkoswald, seven in Renwick and 13 in Staffield. Most of these were owner-occupied and most were within the range 150 a. (60 ha.) and 500 a. (202 ha.), some with large areas of rough grazing on the fellside. Blunderfield East was the last surviving dairy farm in the civil parish of Kirkoswald, all other farmers reared livestock for butchery, with arable production, if any, for animal feed. The Hetheringtons of Staffield Hall farm had acquired a butcher's shop in Penrith to retail beef and lamb produced on their farm.[72]

Woodland and Forestry

In 1568 woodland was recorded within Kirkoswald demesne, Castle Close and Woodhousefield; and in 1606 within Low Maines (Kirkoswald) and two of 35 Staffield tenements described in that survey.[73] In Renwick woodland was owned by the lords of the manor, and the tenants had allowances ('boot') for house-building, fencing and farming implements, and a 'fyre sticke for Christmasse'.[74] During the 17th century, theft of timber by the tenantry was a concern in all three townships, but most of all in Renwick, where in 1690 Archdeacon William Nicolson, acting on behalf of Queen's College, dismissed the bailiff Thomas Gosling because 'he encourag'd many of the trespasses made on your woods'.[75]

In 1860 the Ordnance Survey recorded woodland on about 150 a. (60 ha.) of the Kirkoswald demesnes and parkland, together with areas adjoining the College and the church; 26 a. (10 ha.) of the Huddlesceugh estate; 5 a. (2 ha.) of Viol Moor; and 15 a. (6 ha.) adjoining the Raven Beck in the manor of Haresceugh and Glassonby Beck, and adjoining Cannerheugh farm.[76] In Staffield most woodland was close to the river Eden or Croglin Water, and in Renwick the Raven Beck; and there were patches of woodland in many parts of Staffield, the largest being the 24 a. (10 ha.) Bank Wood on Croglin Hall land: Richard Lowthian Ross planted many thousands of trees in laying out walks on the east bank of Croglin Water.[77] In Staffield 181 a. (73 ha.) of plantation, owned by Fetherstonhaugh, Aglionby and Parkin, were recorded in 1910.[78]

Sir Francis Ley, who purchased the manors of Kirkoswald and Staffield in 1913, paid particular attention to the woodland both for its commercial value and for shooting rights and established a tree nursery in Kirkoswald. In the 1980s, when the farms on the

72 Inf. John and David Hetherington.
73 TNA, SC 11/986.
74 QC, 5A-49 (1616).
75 Manor court rolls: CAS (C), DMUS/1, box 8, Kirkoswald 1620, 1637; CAS (C), DMUS/1/12/1, Staffield 1667; QC, Renwick court book passim and QC, 5A-171.
76 OS Map, 1:10560 Cumb., Sheet XL (1860 edn).
77 CAS (C), Tithe Commutation Schedule 1842, and OS Map, 1:10560 Cumb., Sheets XXXII and XL (1860 edn); Jefferson, *Hist. & Antiq.*, 295.
78 CAS (C), TIR 4/78.

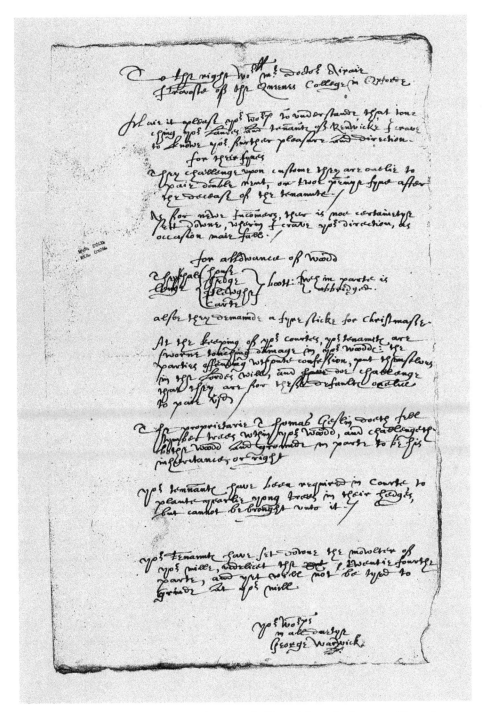

Figure 13 *Letter from George Warwick, steward of Renwick, to the Provost of Queen's College 1616 (QC 5A-49); the letter summarises the main points of contention between the College and their tenantry, including allowances for timber ('boot') and entry fines. Note the 'fyre sticke for Christmasse'.*

former castle parks were sold to the sitting tenants, the woodland was sold separately, specifically for shooting rights. In 2016 it was owned by David Hodgkiss of Nunnery who had embarked on a major programme of felling and replanting.[79]

Mining and Quarrying[80]

In 1620 the tenants of Renwick complained about their neighbours in Staffield taking coal from the Renwick wastes, and in 1630 the Kirkoswald tenants were obliged to provide loads of coal to the lord of the manor. It seems likely that there had been coal mining on the Pennine edge from Tudor times or earlier, but the first formal record was a lease in 1631 of mining rights on Renwick Fell to Anthony Fletcher of Silver Hall, Caldbeck for 40s. per year.[81] The rent was increased to £3 in 1653, £5 in 1691, £10 in 1720, and £33 5s. in 1734 – a rental which remained almost unaltered for 80 years, notwithstanding the opening of Lazonby Bridge over the Eden in 1762, which was expected to improve the market.[82] The mine was said to be worth £40 p.a. in 1688; and was undoubtedly profitable because in 1762 the partners provoked a complaint to a magistrate by purloining from one of their number his document of title.[83] In 1812 the lease was taken by Joseph Dixon of Scalehouses, in partnership with his Walton in-laws, an Alston lead mining family, at £210 per year.[84] There followed a period of greater activity, but by the 1830s there were signs that the seams were nearing exhaustion.[85] The arrival of coal by rail in the 1840s weakened demand for Renwick coal: in 1841 there were eight coal miners in Renwick, but by 1871 none. There was a short-lived revival of coal mining in Renwick in 1899.[86] Neither the thickness nor quality of the seams had been good, but before the arrival of the railways there had been a steady local market and it was used in particular for burning lime 'of the finest and whitest quality' from 1794 (if not earlier) until the 1880s.[87]

Coal mining, lime burning and quarrying also took place on the high fellsides east of Haresceugh and Busk (Kirkoswald) and Scarrowmanwick (Staffield). In 1746 Sir Philip Musgrave leased to Thomas Brown, yeoman of Eamont Bridge, all mines and seams of coal in the manor of Kirkoswald for nine years: from the outset the emphasis was on lime burning, the lessee being obliged to supply Musgrave and his farmers with lime at 3s. ½d. a bushel. In the 1770s the lease was acquired by John Arnison of Selah (d. 1783): it was renewed in 1780, 1783 and 1800.[88] There were clauses (repeated at each renewal)

79   Inf. Timothy Fetherstonhaugh.
80   The author is grateful to Graham Brooks for many of the observations and references in the following passage; see also G. Brooks, 'The East Cumberland Coal Field', *British Mining Memoirs*, no. 88 (Northern Mines Research Society, 2009), 124–36.
81   QC, 5A-53 (1620); CAS (C) DMUS1, box 8 (1630); QC, lease ledger B, 280/1 (1631).
82   QC, lease ledgers D 142, E 267, and F 93; QC, 5A-175 and 5A-105a, a letter from Timothy Fetherstonhaugh esq. to Queen's College, 9 Jan. 1761.
83   Denton, *Perambulation*, 330; CAS (C), D/HUD/8/56.
84   QC, lease ledger J, 103.
85   QC, 5A-159/164.
86   *Diary of John Hall Thompson*, Cumbria Industrial History Society, forthcoming.
87   Hutchinson, *Hist. Cumberland*, I, 212; censuses and trade directories passim.
88   CAS (C), DMUS/5/4/3, box 69 for leases; Hutchinson, *Hist. Cumberland*, I, 204.

Figure 14 *Greenrigg lime kiln, Hartside Fell: locally mined coal and abundant limestone caused many such lime kilns to be built along the Pennine Edge.*

requiring the delivery of coal and lime to the Musgrave lime kilns at Cocklocks. In 1838 land tax was paid for coal and lime works on Haresceugh Fell.[89] Some coal was still being mined in 1860, by which time the Musgrave lime kilns at Cocklocks had been replaced by those at Greenrigg: these were functioning in 1876, but had closed by 1900.[90]

There were extensive limestone quarries at Clint on Scarrowmanwick Fell, and between five and eleven limekilns, fired by coal from Burned Edge coal mine, higher on the Pennine scarp.[91] Lime was carted from Clint to Ewan Close Farm, Lazonby (a distance of ten miles) in the autumn of 1812.[92] A one-third share of the coal mine, together with a one-fourth share of the lime works, part of the estate of John Walton of Highbankhill, who died in 1816, were sold at auction in 1825.[93] Frizzell Hodgson was trading from Scarrowmanwick as a dealer in both coal and lime between 1848 and 1861.[94]

89   CAS (C), PR 9/34, vestry minute 10 Feb. 1838.
90   OS Map, 1:10560 Cumb., Sheet XLI (1860 edn); CAS (C), Q/RE/125; OS Map 1:10560 Cumberland, XLI NW (1900).
91   Graham Brooks (2009, *op cit*) recorded a dry stone adit and a 15-inch thick coal seam; David S. Johnson, 'Lime burning … along the Pennine Edge of Cumberland', *CW3*, XIII (2013), 205 recorded nine kilns.
92   CAS (C), D/HUD/17/107.
93   *Carlisle Jnl*, 10 Sept. 1825.
94   *Slater, Dir. Cumb.* (1848); *P.O., Dir. Cumb.* (1858), 182; *Morris, Harrison & Co., Dir. Cumb.* (1861), 273; OS Map 1:10560 Cumb., Sheet XXXII (1860 edn); Census 1851 (Croglin).

There were freestone quarries in many parts of the manors of all three townships, the largest being Christopher's Quarry near Crindledyke farmhouse (Staffield).[95] Porphyry (marble, blue spotted with white) was extracted at Haresceugh in the first half of the 19th century.[96] An unsuccessful search for copper on the south bank of the Raven Beck downstream from the confluence with Hollgill Beck is recorded as a copper mine, disused by 1860.[97]

Lead and (more productively) barytes were mined on Hartside Fell. A 21-year lease was granted by Sir Philip Musgrave in 1786 to nine lead miners of Alston (in partnership with George Arnison of Selah) to mine for lead ore at Lewgill Head; the lessees were to pay one-seventh part duty ore.[98] It seems that this venture had disappointing results: in 1855 a report by R.R. Maddison and J.C. Cain for the Great Northern Mining Company (GNMC) describes a level driven 'some years ago' for a short distance in a southerly direction before being abandoned. The GNMC were extending exploration, but so far only barytes of a poor quality had been found, and the mine did not seem to be a worthwhile investment.[99] Nevertheless, further efforts were made: when in 1879 the stock of the Hartside Mining Company was put up for sale, it included 100 tons of rails and 48 iron-yard wagons.[100] The mines were reopened north of Busk lime kiln in 1915 by the Hedworth Barium Company, and yielded considerable quantities of high grade barytes: the company built a tramway to carry ore to Hartside Cross, but the works were again abandoned by 1922.[101] Barytes mining was resumed during 1939–45; and in April 1946 the mining rights on Hartside were purchased by Laporte Chemicals, but they appear not to have reopened the mines.[102]

Milling and Manufacturing

Corn Mills

By the 18th century, there were four water corn mills on the Raven Beck operating simultaneously. The lord's mill in Kirkoswald township was recorded in 1399 and 1568, and functioned until 1953.[103] The lord's mill at Renwick, which was recorded in 1404, and Low Huddlesceugh mill, which was recorded in 1619, were both still functioning

---

95   For Christopher's Quarry, see also Staffield Enclosure Award 1816.
96   Hutchinson, *Hist. Cumberland*, I, 204 (Housman's notes); *Parson & White Dir. C&W.* (1829); *Mannix & Whellan, Dir. Cumb.* (1847).
97   OS Map, 1:10560 Cumb., Sheet XXXIII (1860 edn); traces of digging and some abandoned machinery could still be seen onsite in 2016.
98   CAS (C), DMUS/5/3/2, box 69.
99   Letter 5 Mar. 1855 from R.R. Maddison and J.C. Cain; inf. Graham Brookes, from www.aditnow.co.uk, a website with restricted access.
100 *Carlisle Jnl*, 11 Apr. 1879.
101 R.G. Carruthers *et al.* – *Memoirs of the Geological Survey, special report on the mineral resources of Great Britain* vol. II, 'Barytes and Witherite', HMSO, 2nd edn (1922), 38.
102 Some barytes miners died from emphysema due to wartime mining, e.g. John Moses of Renwick who died in 1949 (inf. Nancy Moses).
103 TNA, C 136/109/9, IPM of. William Dacre, 1399; LR 2/213; *Penrith Observer*, 30 Jan. 1953.

in 1879.[104] A fourth, below High Raven Bridge, known as Huddlesceugh Mill (later Ravenbridge Mill), was recorded in 1771 and was still trading in 1881.[105]

Fulling Mills and Textiles

Fulling mills in Kirkoswald were recorded in 1272, 1399, 1568, 1608, 1637, 1675, 1718, and in leases until 1789.[106] From 1675 (and probably long before) there was such a mill on the south bank of the Raven Beck below Tenter Hill, Parkhead. It ceased to be used as a fulling mill in 1789 (see paper mills below); its ruins and a disused mill race could still be seen in 2016.[107] Fulling mills were required to finish the cloth produced by cottage weavers, also doubtless widespread in all three townships from the 14th century. Joseph Hamilton (1796–1875, of Highbankhill), was recorded as a handloom weaver in 1829, 1841 and 1851, a carpet weaver in 1861 and a woollen weaver in 1871.[108] Dyers are recorded in Kirkoswald from 1690. Industrialised textile production in Kirkoswald began in the 1840s. William Carr, a Haltwhistle man, was recorded as a dyer in 1841, and from 1847 to 1861 was operating a small woollen mill, building up to three employees in 1861.[109] He was succeeded by his nephew William Threlkeld (1833–1904) who, with his son, continued the business into the 20th century. Their mill, the former paper mill on the east bank of the Raven, acquired by lease in 1883, ceased to be used for textile manufacture in 1906 and later became a saw mill.[110]

Papermaking

Paper mills are recorded in Kirkoswald from 1715 to 1881. Thomas Rickerby (d. 1724) was manufacturing paper in 1715, but this enterprise ended with his death.[111] Joseph Smith (d. 1723) manufactured paper in competition with Rickerby, and his son Bartholomew continued the business, acquired rights to additional water in 1737, and in 1741 was admonished by the consistory court for working the mill on the Sabbath. He sold the mill to Thomas Dixon and James Dobson in 1755.[112] In 1789 William Crampton (d. 1825) was granted a lease of the fulling mill with the obligation to rebuild and equip it for the making of paper: he was succeeded by his son Joseph, who in 1828 was granted the lease of a newly erected paper mill with machinery and engines but was bankrupted in 1831.[113]

104 QC, Long Rolls 1404; TNA, E 134/1619; *Dir. Cumb.* to 1879.
105 CAS (C), PROB/1771/W1329, will of William Greenop, 1771; Census 1881.
106 TNA, C 132/42/4, IPM of Helewisa de Levynton, 1272; C 136/109/9, IPM of William Dacre, 1399; SC 11/986/1; Kirkoswald manor court 1637, 1675; ERO, Barrett-Lennard, M79/4 (1718); CAS (C), DMUS, box 69, for leases to 1789.
107 OS Map, 1:2500 Cumb., Sheet XL-6 (1900 edn), fields 260, 267, field names from Tithe Schedule 1842; Eden, *State of the Poor*, 84, mentions one dyer and one fuller in Kirkoswald.
108 *Parson & White, Dir. C&W* (1829), 491; censuses passim.
109 Census, 1841, 1861; *Mannix & Whellan, Dir. Cumb.* (1847), 280; *P.O., Dir. Cumb* (1858), 182; *Morris, Harrison & Co., Dir. Cumb.* (1861), 272.
110 Census, 1861–1901; *Dir. Cumb.* 1879–1901; OS Map, 1:2500 Cumb., Sheet XL-6 (1900 edn); CAS (C), DMUS/2/4, box 27; see saw mills below.
111 CAS (C), DMUS/1/6, box 8, Kirkoswald manor court, 1715–25.
112 Ibid., 1737; DRC 5/7 (1741); Fetherstonhaugh, A-24-7.
113 *Parson & White, Dir. C&W* (1829), 491; *The Morning Post*, 31 Dec. 1831. This mill, on the east side of the Raven, was shown as a paper mill on OS Map 1:10560 Cumb., Sheet XL (1860 edn), and as a woollen mill on OS Map, 1:2500 Cumberland, Sheet XL-6 (1900 edn).

William Hastings, a Devonian, manufactured paper in Kirkoswald from 1850 until 1861: in 1856 he installed a vortex water wheel manufactured by McAdam of Belfast.[114] In the 1870s the paper mill was purchased by Roberts & Parker, who also operated a mill at Glassonby Beck to which they eventually transferred their activities: the Kirkoswald paper mill was offered for sale, together with a steam engine, in 1882.[115] The manufacture of paper required an excise officer in Kirkoswald, recorded from 1725 until 1881.[116] The number of Kirkoswald residents employed in papermaking reached a peak of 11 in 1861.[117]

Saw Mills and Woodworking

William Richardson (1814–94) was operating both a corn mill and a saw mill in Kirkoswald in 1846 and described himself as a timber merchant.[118] In 1851 he increased supplies of water to his mill. By 1861 he had widened his range of activities to include bobbin-making and candlewick manufacture.[119] In 1866 he was advertising his saw mills at Kirkoswald and Plumpton in a Manchester newspaper.[120] The Kirkoswald bobbin industry ended in 1873, but Richardson was still trading as a timber merchant in 1884.[121] After his purchase of the manor in 1913, Sir Francis Ley adapted Threlkeld's woollen mill to a saw mill, together with a pressure creosoting plant, the first in England north of Preston.[122] At a later date the power source was changed to electricity, and in 2016 the mill and its equipment were still there, if seldom used.

Brewing

A brewery was established in what is now Ravenghyll, Kirkoswald in 1833 by William Holliday, who supplied many public and private houses in the area but went out of business in 1841.[123] The brewery was continued until 1867 by John Walton, publican of the George and Dragon,[124] and, later, William Hodgson of the Crown Hotel: it ceased to trade in the early 1880s.[125]

---

114 CAS (C), DMUS/2, box 27.

115 Census, 1851–91; *P.O., Dir. Cumb.* (1858), 182; *Morris, Harrison & Co., Dir. Cumb.* (1861), 272; *Slater, Dir. Cumb.* (1879), 118; CAS (C), DMUS/2, box 27 (letter 1882).

116 CAS (C), PR 9 series (church registers 1725–1840).

117 Census, 1861.

118 CAS (C), DMUS/2, box 27; *Mannix and Whellan, Dir. Cumb.* (1847), 280; baptism 1843; Census 1851.

119 Fetherstonhaugh, A-24-59; *P.O., Dir. Cumb.* (1858), 182; for bobbin mill workers, baptisms from 1856; Census, 1861 (6), 1871 (17).

120 *Manchester Guardian*, 14 Feb. 1866.

121 *Liverpool Mercury*, 9 Aug. 1873; *Bulmer, Dir. Cumb.* (1884), 591.

122 Inf. Timothy Fetherstonhaugh.

123 CAS (C), DMUS/10, box 122; the brewery is marked on OS Map, 1:2500, Cumb., XL-6 (1890 edn).

124 *Slater, Dir. Cumb.* (1848), 143; Census 1851; CAS (C), DMUS/2/4, box 27, sale of malt kiln, 1867.

125 *P.O., Dir. Cumb.* (1858), 182; *Morris, Harrison & Co., Dir. Cumb.* (1861), 272; *Slater, Dir. Cumb.* (1879), 116; but not 1884; Census, 1861–81.

Markets, Fairs and Commerce

Hugh de Morville received a grant of the right to hold a weekly market and annual fair in Kirkoswald in 1201.[126] During the time of Crown and Lennard lordship (1570–1716), the market was controlled by the manor court and held on Thursday each week: there was also a fair yearly upon St Oswald's Day (5 Aug.).[127] In 1718 the Musgraves leased the tolls and shambles for one guinea p.a., and in 1752, for the same rent, 'the shambles and all the profits and advantages arising from the fairs and markets there'. From 1774 to 1823 the tolls of fairs and shambles were included in leases of Demesne Farm, and in 1816 the market was 'only for butcher's meat'.[128] In 1829 neither the ancient market (Thursday) nor the corn market (Monday) were in a prosperous state; and the market had been discontinued by 1858, though fairs were still held twice a year.[129] A spring fair, for livestock, was held in 1864, but seems thereafter to have been replaced by an annual Kirkoswald agricultural and/or horticultural show.[130]

It may be that the market enhanced the attractiveness of the township for retail outlets and as a central place in which a range of local trades and professions could be practised: in addition to the ubiquitous trades of smithing, joinery, stonemasonry, tailoring, shoemaking and weaving, there were in Kirkoswald (with first recorded dates) coopers (1608), butchers (1713), bakers (1741), and nine other manufacturing trades; medical practitioners are recorded from 1793 and veterinary surgeons from 1841.[131] The many inns and taverns also reflect the function of Kirkoswald as a central place. There was more than one public house in Kirkoswald in 1629.[132] By 1753 the number exceeded ten, including those outside the village.[133] In 1822 there were six in Kirkoswald village alone, namely, the Bluebell, the Black Swan, the Black Bull, the Crown, the King's Head and the George and Dragon.[134] The Fetherston Arms was built on the site of the Bluebell in 1826; and no more is heard of the Black Swan.[135] In 1829 there were five public houses, all grouped around or close to the Market Square; and taverns at Haresceugh ('Horse Head') and Selah ('Board Inn').[136] The latter had ceased to trade by 1847, and the King's Head before 1910. The principal inns were the George and Dragon which ceased to trade

126 *Rot. Chart.*, 89; http://www.history.ac.uk/cmh/gaz/gazweb2.html (accessed 1 Sept. 2017).
127 CAS (C), DMUS/1/3/1 (undated *c.*1630); and manor court rolls 1620, 1667.
128 CAS (C), DMUS/5/4/3, box 70; Lysons, *Magna Britannia: Cumb.*, 128.
129 *Parson & White, Dir. C&W* (1829), 490; *Mannix & Whellan, Dir. Cumb.* (1847), 278; *P.O., Dir. Cumb.* (1858), 181.
130 *Cumberland and Westmorland Herald,* 19 Apr. 1864; see also Soc. Hist.
131 Kirkoswald church registers and title deeds, passim.
132 CAS (C), DMUS/1/3/1.
133 CAS (C), Q/L/2/1; one was called the King's Arms (manor court, 1743, 1752); and another the Boot and Shoe: *Cumberland Pacquet*, 30 Nov. 1784; the George (later George and Dragon) and the Black Bull hosted meetings of the two friendly societies in the 1790s: see also Soc. Hist.
134 CAS (C), Q/L/3/6; for the George and Dragon see also Kirkoswald manor court roll 1796, and CAS (K), WD/CAT/A2095 (1816).
135 *Carlisle Jnl,* 19 Aug. 1826; for the Bluebell CAS (C), Q/L/3/6 (1823/5); Fetherstonhaugh, A-19-45 (1817), purchase by C.S. Fetherstonhaugh.
136 *Parson & White, Dir. C&W* (1829), 492 omitting the George and Dragon.

between 1905 and 1910;[137] the Black Bull which in 1916 was acquired from Miss Rachel Graham by the Carlisle & District State Management Scheme and ceased trading in 1991;[138] and the Fetherston Arms and the Crown which were still trading in 2016.

A dealer's shop was recorded in Kirkoswald in 1606.[139] Later in the 17th century and in the first part of the 18th century there were at least four shops. Henry Bird (1654–1733) sold two shops to Bartholomew Smith (d. 1697) in 1680: Smith was selling (*inter alia*) sugar in 1693, and after his death the business was continued first by his son Joseph Smith (d. 1723), and then by his grandson Bartholomew until his departure from Kirkoswald in 1750.[140] Thomas Henderson (d. 1684) was a 'grocer' with two retail outlets; he was succeeded by his son Joseph (d. 1713, 'merchant' 1698), and his grandson George who sold to Joseph Smith in 1719.[141] Later in the 18th century and continuing into the early 19th century Joseph Bell (1737–94), Joseph Johnston (1768–1824), and William and Joseph Dodd are all recorded as grocers and shopkeepers.[142] In 1829 six men and

Figure 15 *One of several general stores in Kirkoswald before 1900, this building stands at the junction of Kirkoswald High Street, with the road to Staffield to the left and the road to Renwick to the right; it is now used as a workshop.*

137 Tiffin, *Memories of Kirkoswald*; no mention in *Kelly's Dir. C&W.* (1910), 192 nor Census 1911.
138 TNA, HO 190/200, and local inf.
139 TNA, SC 11/986.
140 CAS (C), DMUS/1/6/1/3, Kirkoswald manor court 1680, 1693, 1697, 1724; Fetherstonhaugh, A-24-1, A-6-1, A-24-4.
141 CAS (C), DMUS/1/12/1 (Staffield Manor Court 29 Oct. 1683); PROB/1685/AINVX36 (inventory of Thomas Henderson, 1684); baptism 1686.
142 Baptisms and burials 1774–1824; Fetherstonhaugh, B-3-8 1816; *Carlisle Patriot*, 18 May 1822 for bankruptcy of Joseph and William Dodd grocers, ironmongers, woollen goods and drapery.

women were listed as grocers, drapers and/or shopkeepers. Their shop fronts mingled with those of a butcher, a baker, a cooper, a nailer, a saddler, three blacksmiths, three shoemakers, three joiners, three tailors, and two wine and spirit merchants.[143] By 1851 there was also a post office and all the trades present in 1829, together with the woollen mill, paper mill and saw mill.[144] In 1865 the Cumberland Union Banking Company opened their Kirkoswald branch in a new three-storey building with an Italianate frontage on the north-east corner of the market place. It was acquired by Midland Bank in 1918 and closed in 1983.[145] However, in 1884, Kirkoswald was described as a 'place of very little trade'.[146]

By 1901, the decline of Kirkoswald as a central place had begun. A bank, post office, five public houses, and corn and woollen mills survived, but there were now only three grocers, a saddler, a smith, two joiners, three butchers, two tailors, a shoemaker and a wine merchant. The inhabitants, it was said, were 'chiefly engaged in agriculture, although a few find employment in a small woollen factory and carding mill'; seven Kirkoswald men were employed as gypsum miners at Long Meg mines (Glassonby), and another seven on the Carlisle–Settle railway (Lazonby).[147] In 1938 there were a bank, a post office, three shops, three public houses, a corn mill, a smith, a joiner and a butcher, while Howard Lace was a motor engineer and bus operator based in a former smithy.[148]

In 1945 four shops still remained in Kirkoswald, and in 1977 the Cranstons, who had worked a small abattoir in Sandhill since the 1920s, opened a butcher's shop in Sandhill.[149] The Todd family, builders and contractors of Highbankhill, were the largest employers of labour in Kirkoswald in the 1970s.[150] In 2016 there remained one general store and newsagent (with volunteer staff), two public houses, a doctors' surgery, a saw mill (infrequently used) and Lace's motor garage.

Service Industries in Renwick Village

Renwick also housed shops, tradesmen and inns, particularly during the period of intensive coal mining from 1812 to 1850. There may have been an inn in Renwick from about 1620: Bernard Westmorland (d. 1630), who seems to have been a victualler, acquired a plot of freehold land, formerly demesne, which later included the site of the Horse and Jockey Inn.[151] It was sold to Richard Beckton whose descendants traded there as publicans until the 1840s;[152] the inn was enlarged in about 1800 and the manor courts

143 *Parson & White, Dir. C&W* (1829), 492.
144 *Mannix and Whellan, Dir. Cumb.* (1847), 280–1; Census 1851.
145 Archives of Hong Kong and Shanghai Bank, UK G 007, with thanks to Jemma Lee; *Slater, Dir. Cumb.* (1879), 69; Census 1881.
146 *Slater, Dir. Cumb.* (1884), 120.
147 Census 1901, 1911; *Bulmer, Dir. Cumb.* (1901), 413; for Long Meg mines see also Fetherstonhaugh, *Our Cumberland Village*, 78 and Tiffin, *Memories of Kirkoswald*.
148 *Kelly's Dir. C&W* (1938), 196.
149 Oral evidence of Bunty Cranston, Bob Parker, Mike Clementson; inf. John Haugh, Neville Jackson; in 2016 Cranstons owned large retail outlets in several towns, but no longer Kirkoswald.
150 Inf. Tom Bowman, Timothy Fetherstonhaugh.
151 QC, 5A-23, court roll, 1603; 5A-37, call roll of freeholders, 1647.
152 QC, Renwick court book 41.

were held there from 1803 to 1816.[153] In the 1890s it was purchased and further enlarged by Joseph Nicholson, and as part of the Ravenwood estate continued to trade until 1953.[154] A second inn, the Black Bull, was opened by the Head family at the east end of the village in the 1820s and was still trading in 1871;[155] a third and a fourth were opened in the 1830s, perhaps in response to the Beer Act 1830, in newly erected buildings on land enclosed in 1818 on the south side of the former village green. One traded for only ten years, but the Queen's College Inn was still trading in 1901.[156] In the 1830s all four Renwick inns were buying beer from William Holliday's brewery at Kirkoswald.[157]

Throughout the three townships it was usual before 1750 for trades to be practised as an adjunct to farming. The first Renwick men to be routinely described by their trade were Anthony Sowerby (1717–1801, a blacksmith), Jonathan Watson (1734–97, a tailor), and Paul Richardson (1742–99, a stonemason). Sowerby was granted a small freehold intake on which to build a smithy in 1752.[158] There were plentiful sources of freestone (red sandstone) in the parish and many Renwick men were employed in stone masonry, walling and housebuilding, the Watson family being prominent from the 1690s to about 1900. The Lowthians of Sickergill described themselves as maltsters in 1782.[159] Henry Moses described himself as a grocer in 1818: in 1829 he was a schoolmaster and shopkeeper.[160]

Business activity in Renwick expanded with coal mining after 1812. Coal and lime had to be transported, by packhorse or cart, off the fells to markets and customers; and blacksmiths prospered: in 1851 there were four blacksmiths in Renwick, but before 1800, and after 1901, only one.[161] By 1851 three grocers were established in Renwick, by 1861 four, by 1911 three (one of whom was postmistress), but the last grocery shop in Renwick closed in about 1970.[162] There was a post office in Renwick from 1901, and in 2016 it still functioned on two half days a week. John Frost made clocks and watches in Renwick between 1815 and his death in 1841.[163] Isaac Robinson (1818–87) established a tailoring business in Renwick which was still trading in the 1930s; and a haulage and motor garage traded between the 1930s and 1960s.[164]

In Staffield, joinery, weaving, brewing, malting and tanning are all recorded in probate inventories and court rolls in the 16th and 17th centuries, probably small businesses meeting local needs and supplementing farming income.[165] The tannery at Netherharesceugh, operated by Edmund Bird from about 1680 to his death in 1723, was a larger business. Bird acquired and (in 1701) extended Netherharesceugh farmhouse, purchased land both in Kirkoswald and elsewhere, and at his death had an inventory of

153 QC, 5A-191, Renwick manor court, 1803–16.
154 Date stone 'JN 1892'; title deeds of Castle House, Renwick (Mrs A. St John).
155 Trade directories passim.
156 *Bulmer, Dir. Cumb.* (1901), 470; Census 1901, household 28.
157 CAS (C), DMUS/10/122.
158 Church registers for descriptions; QC, Renwick court book 240 (1752) for smithy.
159 QC, 5A-114.
160 Methodist Chapel trust deed 1818 (at Kirkoswald manse); *Parson & White, Dir. C&W* (1829), 511.
161 Census 1851 for Renwick, households 14, 21, 43, 56; *P.O., Dir. Cumb.* (1858), 201.
162 Census 1841–1911, passim; trade directories 1847–1938, passim; local inf.
163 J.B. Penfold, *The Clockmakers of Cumberland* (Ashford, 1977), 202.
164 *Bulmer, Dir. Cumb.* (1884), 122; local inf. Stanley and Hardy Greenop.
165 Staffield wills and inventories, passim.

over £3,800.[166] In 1670 a blacksmith called John Bownus was allowed to erect a cottage 'upon the common by the wayside' at Highbankhill, with a rent of 1*d*. In 1680 this smithy and shop were sold to William Coulthard, who worked the smithy for at least 39 years.[167] John Lawrence of Staffield was recorded as a smith in 1693 and 1703.[168] In 1797 George Dixon and his son Robert had established a new smithy in the hamlet of Staffield, which was worked by three generations of Dixons until 1871, and by William Bowes in 1884, but had ceased trading by 1891.[169] In 1797 Staffield also had two shoemakers, one stonemason and one weaver.[170] Joseph Lawrence, and his sons Thomas and Joseph, were shoemakers in Staffield between 1775 and 1853. The Irving family were trading as bacon factors at Burnt House from 1841 to 1891. The Watson family traded as stonemasons at Highbankhill until 1871, and Thomas Chambers was working as a stonemason with two apprentices at Westgarthhill in 1881.[171] The Joiner's Arms was trading as an inn in 1779 and last recorded in 1884.[172] A public house called the Ship Inn traded between about 1840 and 1865 at what was in 2016 Scarrowmanwick farmhouse.[173]

In 1921 Richard Denman, who had recently purchased the Staffield Hall estate, constructed a small hydro-electric plant on Croglin Water, near the top waterfall in Nunnery Walks. By so doing he supplied electricity (direct current) to Staffield Hall and the cottages of Staffield hamlet, some 20 years before the main network of supply reached Staffield.[174] The scheme was designed, and the machinery manufactured, by Gilkes of Kendal: it incorporated a small dam and a tunnel (dug by miners) to deliver the water to a Francis turbine. The builders were the Clementsons of Kirkoswald.[175]

Tourism has touched the parish of Kirkoswald lightly. In the 1960s and 1970s fishermen visited Kirkoswald for salmon fishing in the Eden.[176] Licences to fish in the river Eden were once issued from the Fetherston Arms, but in 2016 the fishing rights were privately licensed to local people. A caravan park with stands for 12 caravans and a camping ground was established by Robert and Julie Pickthall at Mains Farm in 2008, close to the 'Coast to Coast' cycle route, and in 2016 this business had grown to 28 sites, an enlarged camping site and camping 'pods', with showering and cooking facilities in converted barns. The Crown and Fetherston Arms Inns both derived increased custom

---

166 CAS (C), PROB/1723/WINVX12, will and inventory of Edmund Bird, 1723.
167 CAS (C), DMUS/1/12/1, rentals 1670, 1675, 1680; two admittances and call rolls to 1719.
168 Baptisms; datestone 'ILM 1702' on cottage in Staffield, is John and Mary Lawrence.
169 Eden, *State of the Poor*, 83–4; baptisms from 1803. In 1946 Sir Richard Denman applied for planning permission to convert the old smithy to a cottage: CAS (C), SRPD/3/PLANS/265l.
170 Eden, *State of the Poor*, 83–4.
171 *Census* 1801–91; *Parson & White, Dir. C&W* (1829), 492; *Mannix & Whellan, Dir. Cumb.* (1847), 281; *Slater, Dir. Cumb.* (1869), 69; baptism records Kirkoswald and Ainstable.
172 Baptism 1779; CAS (C), Q/L/3/6 (1822/5); *Parson & White, Dir. C&W* (1829), 492; *Mannix & Whellan, Dir. Cumb.* (1847), 281; *Morris, Harrison & Co., Dir. Cumb.* (1861), 273; *Slater, Dir. Cumb.* (1879 & 1884), 117, 122; Census 1801–81; OS Map 1:10560 Cumb., Sheet XL (1860 edn), one of the cottages in Staffield hamlet.
173 Inf. Robin Bell; *Mannix and Whellan, Dir. Cumb.* (1847), 281; Census 1861.
174 *Cumberland and Westmorland Herald*, 1920.
175 Inf. Gilkes & Co. Ltd., drawings 2376 and 2463, with thanks to Alastair Steele (Gilkes) and Mrs Kathy Cowburn, daughter of Sir Richard and Lady May Denman; Clementson business records in custody of Michael Clementson.
176 Inf. Neville Jackson.

in their bars and restaurants from these initiatives. In addition, self-catering holiday accommodation was available at Howscales, Kirkoswald;[177] part of Staffield Hall was converted after 1995 to eight holiday apartments; six holiday cottages were established by Richard and Sue Bottom at Crossfield House.[178]

Between 1945 and 2016 Kirkoswald became increasingly a village of commuters, and in all three townships residents employed on the land or otherwise became outnumbered by those who worked elsewhere. Economic activity based on the place of residence is exemplified by the case of Thomas Edward Hughes, an internationally renowned potter specialising in Japanese styles, who operated a pottery in Renwick from 1984 to 1989. Most of his production was exported to Japan where his styles were much in demand and fetched high prices.[179]

177 Inf. Robert and Julie Pickthall.
178 Inf. Richard and Sue Bottom and George Stobart.
179 *The Times*, 29 Apr. 2006, obituary. The author thanks David Cross for drawing attention to T.E. Hughes and his Renwick pottery.

SOCIAL HISTORY

THE POPULATION OF KIRKOSWALD has for most of its recorded history included a resident social elite – the baronial family of Dacre (who were lords of the manors of Kirkoswald and Staffield) to 1566, and the Fetherstonhaughs (who were not) after 1611. At the level of local administration and vestry government (until 1894), farmers dominated throughout the area of study, but power was shared in Kirkoswald itself by prosperous tradesmen. Although Kirkoswald township, with its market and shopping centre, would have fulfilled many social needs for the peoples of Staffield and Renwick, both those townships retained significant independence, until the centralising reforms of the 19th and 20th centuries. Renwick had its own school from 1758 to 1987; and administered the Poor Law until 1836, as did Staffield from 1708.

Social Structure and Character

Kirkoswald Castle, enlarged and improved by Thomas, 2nd Baron Dacre of the North in about 1500, is thought to have been the preferred baronial residence from then to the death of Thomas, 4th Baron Dacre in 1566, during which time social life in Kirkoswald was no doubt dominated by the barons and their retainers.[1] After 1566 there was no resident lord of the manor, apart from the Crown lessee Thomas Bartram (d. 1639) who from 1606 resided at Demesne Farm, effectively then the manor house.[2] Henry Fetherstonhaugh (d. 1626), who purchased the College in 1611, was the royal steward of several adjacent manors and had serious disagreements with Bartram.[3] His son, Sir Timothy Fetherstonhaugh (1601–51, knighted in 1628) was, after Bartram's death, the squire of Kirkoswald, active in county affairs and a vigorous supporter of royal policy.[4] His execution in 1651, and the financial and other consequences of the civil wars, reduced his family's influence for a generation during and after the interregnum, but by the 1690s their wealth and influence were largely restored.[5] During the following 300 years, the Fetherstonhaughs, although not lords of the manor, were a resident gentry presence in the village, fulfilling many of the gentry roles: they were usually magistrates, and served (from the 19th century) as poor law guardians and local councillors, and, through younger sons and brothers, as village officers.[6] Charles Smalwood

---

1 The 3rd and 4th barons both died at Kirkoswald (1563 and 1566).
2 Hyde & Pevsner, *Cumbria*, 477 refers to Demesne farmhouse as the Manor House.
3 Fetherstonhaugh, A-20-8 (arbitration 1622).
4 *ODNB*, s.v., Fetherstonhaugh, Sir Timothy (1601–51) (accessed 1 Mar. 2017).
5 Fetherstonhaugh, A-20-9 (1708 account); see also *Cal. Cttee. for Compounding*, pt. 3, p. 1669.
6 CAS (C), PR 9/5, from 1707.

Figure 16 *Portrait
(artist unknown)
of Sir Timothy
Fetherstonhaugh,
executed at Chester in
October 1651.*

Fetherstonhaugh (1762–1839), and his son Timothy Fetherstonhaugh (1811–56) were both active in community affairs, frequently chairing meetings, and adjudicating issues arising from vestry disputes.[7] Colonel Timothy Fetherstonhaugh (1869–1945), the author of *Our Cumberland Village*, chaired the Kirkoswald parish council and school managers for many years, and also the Penrith bench of magistrates and Cumberland Quarter Sessions, of which he was the last lay chairman. His son Timothy (1899–1969), who was knighted for political services, was a Cumberland county councillor, member of the police authority, and treasurer of the Kirkoswald Church Institute and parochial church council; his wife was president of the Kirkoswald Women's Institute, while their son Timothy (b. 1936) served on Penrith Rural District Council from 1967 to 1974, Eden District Council from 1974 to 2000, and Kirkoswald parish council from 1967 to 2005. There were periods when the heads of the family were absent from Kirkoswald – notably between 1873 and 1909, during which the College was leased to James Mark Wood of Liverpool.[8]

7   E.g. CAS (C), PR 9/34, undated end page, a poor law settlement matter.
8   Fetherstonhaugh, A-14-6, lease to Marke Wood, 1888; inf. Timothy Fetherstonhaugh.

At times other gentry were resident in Kirkoswald and Staffield. The resident owners of Huddlesceugh Hall until the late 17th century, the Hutton and Barwis families, were usually described as gentry, as were the Towry family who were resident at Croglin (Low) Hall from 1660 to 1733.[9] George Lowthian of Staffield (d. 1735) was referred to as 'gent',[10] and it was he who renamed his customary farmhold 'Staffield Hall': after 1750 this family were irregularly resident in Staffield, but a great-grandson Richard Lowthian Ross settled there after 1800 as a gentry figure, and in the 1890s Arthur Charles Aglionby lived there.[11] From 1848 to 1885 Charles Fetherstonhaugh (a younger son of the Kirkoswald family) and his wife Jane Aglionby, lived with their large household at the newly built Staffield Hall.[12] From 1920 to 1975 Staffield Hall was owned and occupied by the Hon Richard Denman and his wife (later Sir Richard and Lady [May] Denman).

Use of the honorific 'Mr' to recognise relative wealth hints at the social separation of some non-gentry families. In both Kirkoswald and Staffield this usage was adopted in the 17th century by some of the larger farmers: for example, in Kirkoswald, William Bowman (d. 1620), Oswald Bird (d. 1658) and his son John (d. 1706),[13] and in Staffield during the 1660s and 1670s, Richard Wilson of Crossfield.[14] From the 1730s some of the larger freeholders in Staffield – the Threlkelds of Caber, the Westmorlands of Scales Hall, the Lowthians of Netherharesceugh, the Moresbys of Westgarthhill, the Whitwhams of Blunderfield and the Robleys of Scarrowmanwick – were returned for county jury service, and were sometimes described as 'Mr'.[15] The honorific was also applied to a few successful tradesmen, including merchants, such as Joseph Henderson (d. 1713) and Edward Thornbarrow (d. 1748), and the prosperous tanner Edmund Bird (d. 1723).[16] In Renwick, where use of the honorific was infrequent, it was applied to Thomas Sowerby (d. 1728), the impropriator and patron of Renwick church.[17]

In all three townships farmers filled most of the manor and township offices. Before 1650 the foremanship of the Kirkoswald and Staffield manor court juries were shared by several men, but after the Restoration the Threlkelds of Caber became increasingly dominant in both manors. Tradesmen occasionally presided: for example, Edmund Bird of Staffield in 1684, and Bartholomew Smith of Kirkoswald in 1682, 1688 and 1691. Kirkoswald vestry included Staffield farmers until 1708, after which Staffield assumed separate administration.[18]

In Renwick, where freeholders and customary tenants appear to have shared the positions of responsibility equally and in rotation, no dominant family dynasties existed before the late 18th century: men who were prominent in the years leading up to enclosure in 1818 were Robert Monkhouse of Scalehouses (d. 1791) and his son John

9   *Pedigrees Visitations*, 135 (Towry of Croglin Hall).
10   E.g. Staffield manor court call rolls from 1694.
11   Lysons, *Magna Britannia: Cumb.*, 128; Census 1891, 1901 and *Dir. Cumb.* passim. For Arthur Charles Aglionby, above, Landownership (Staffield Hall).
12   Census, 1851; *Dir. Cumb.* passim.
13   Burial 1620; Kirkoswald manor court 1659; baptism 1693.
14   TNA, E 179/367/2, Hearth Tax return, 1662.
15   CAS (C), Q/RJ/2.
16   Fetherstonhaugh, A-20-28 ('Mr' Joseph Henderson, 1691); CAS (C), PR 9/5, passim; baptism 1701.
17   CAS (C), PR 9/2, Renwick burial register, 1723, 1728.
18   CAS (C), PR 9/5; Q/6/1, 512; see Local Govt. below.

(d. 1856), William Lowson (d. 1819, the patron of the church), Jonathan Tallentire of Outhwaite (d. 1815) and John Lowthian of Sickergill (d. 1826). From 1873 (when he acquired the patronage of the church), Joseph Nicholson of Ravenwood was accepted as squire of Renwick, a status inherited in 1895 by his heir William Salkeld and in 1935 by George Wilfred Armstrong.[19] The squirarchy ended with Armstrong's death in 1956.

Servants and Cottagers

Elizabethan and Stuart wills occasionally mention servants, and the larger houses employed many.[20] Several cottagers lived in Kirkoswald and Staffield on both customary and freehold land, and on the wastes.[21] Before 1660 only one cottage was recorded in Renwick, but the number rose steadily thereafter.[22] In 1841, in the three townships, there were 114 in-servants and 113 cottages, occupied by agricultural labourers, coal miners and tradesmen, their families and single ladies (more than half the population of 1,267), with concentrations of cottages at Haresceugh, Viol Moor, Kirkoswald Town End, Renwick village and Staffield hamlet. Most servants were employed on farms and at the College, Kirkoswald. The construction of Staffield Hall in 1848 created a second household with large numbers of domestic staff.[23] In 1901 there were 81 servants on farms, 53 domestic servants, and 45 labourers in their own homes.[24]

Community Activities

A Friendly Society was founded at Kirkoswald in 1758. It published rules and orders in 1794, and was holding meetings at the George and Dragon Inn in 1825. A second Friendly Society, at first called 'Kirkoswald Union Society', was founded in 1783.[25] A Book Club, founded in 1816 by officer of excise John Dobson, was in 1870 referred to as the Kirkoswald Literary Institution, and in 1925 as 'one of the oldest institutions of the parish'.[26] A reading room and library had been established by 1882 in the street now called Ravenghyll, a single-storey building with a panelled interior. Annual concerts in its aid were held there in the 1880s with entertainment by 'the best of the talent of the district'; a similar event was held at the National School seven weeks later in aid of school

---

19   The squirearchy is evidenced by collective memory, and the holding of offices such as patronage of the church and chairmanship of school managers.

20   CAS (C), PROB/1622/WX122, the will of Richard Rumney (1622), an employee of Henry Fetherstonhaugh, mentions four women servants and 'every one of my master's menservants'.

21   TNA, SC 11/986 (four cottages in Kirkoswald, 1606); Staffield rental 1675 (two cottages); CAS (C), DX8/1/1 (witness statement 1703 'there are several cottages built on Staffall wastes').

22   QC, 5A-13 (1598) and Renwick court book, passim.

23   Staffield census 1851, household 34, 7 servants.

24   Census, 1901.

25   CAS (C), D/HOD/11/158/160.

26   Fetherstonhaugh, *Our Cumberland Village*, 78; Dobson was drowned in the river Eden: *Lancaster Gaz.*, 18 Jan. 1817; CAS (C), DX 1076/1, letter of recommendation of Caleb Watson, secretary of three local societies, 1870.

repairs.[27] By 1945 the building was no longer used as a reading room: it was later used by the scouts and guides, and converted to a private house in 1988.[28]

The Kirkoswald Lazonby and District Floral and Horticultural Society held its third annual meeting (followed by a cricket match) at Kirkoswald in 1862;[29] and in 1874 a Kirkoswald flower fruit and vegetable show was held in the castle precincts with music and dancing to the Garrigill Brass Band.[30] The following year the Kirkoswald Agricultural Society held an inaugural meeting at the George Hotel Kirkoswald; and under its aegis there was a floral and horticultural exhibition in the castle precincts in September with musical entertainment, as in 1874.[31] The Agricultural Society held annual shows from the 1880s, probably on what would later be called the Old Show Field, on the western edge of the village.[32] These were continued until 1932 and, having

Figure 17 *The College, Kirkoswald, seen from the west, with the river Eden behind the camera; photograph published by the* Cumberland and Westmorland Herald *on 9 September 1950, to record an Agricultural Show on the College lawns.*

27   *Penrith Herald*, 4 Dec. 1886, 21 Jan. 1887.
28   *Kelly's Dir. C&W* (1938), 186; inf. Timothy Fetherstonhaugh and Ruth Lee.
29   *Cumberland &Westmorland Herald*, 2 Sept. 1862.
30   *Cumberland & Westmorland Herald*, 1 Sept. 1874.
31   *Cumberland & Westmorland Herald*, 9 Mar. 1875, 15 Sept. 1875.
32   *Cumberland & Westmorland Herald*, 9 Sept. 1882, 6 Oct. 1883, 4 Sept. 1888, 25 Aug. 1896 and 10 Aug. 1901.

been revived in 1948, were held annually until 1967 on the first Saturday in September on the College Lawn (see Fig. 17).[33]

A cricket club, first recorded in 1863 using Kelsey Syke (the Church Holme) as a playing ground, was functioning in 1913, but ceased activity in wartime. There was a revival in 1921 for a few years; and again from 1934 to 1939, as Staffield Cricket Club using a field adjoining the Nunnery. In 1946 Staffield Cricket Club was again revived, retaining the name but using the Old Show Field at Kirkoswald. A small hut in use from 1946 was replaced by a pavilion in 1989.[34] A football club, first recorded in 1922, also played on the Church Holme for a few years. It was restarted in 1946, and for some years ran a 'medals competition' (the profits of which were used to give Kirkoswald schoolchildren a day trip to Morecambe), before being disbanded in the early 1960s. It was restarted in 1969 at the Old Show Field, which it shared with the cricket club, and both remained active in 2016 competing in county leagues.[35]

In 1897 there were also in Kirkoswald (besides the societies and clubs already mentioned) a tennis club, a Sons of Temperance Friendly Society and a branch of the Manchester Unity Society of Oddfellows.[36] Community events, such as concerts, were held at the reading room or the school until 1910 when the Church Institute (a single-storey building with large hall and small meeting room) was built by the heirs of James Mark Wood, lessee of the College. In 1925 the Book Club and a Recreation Club (and billiard table) were based at the Institute.[37] A Sports Day was held at Haresceugh on 4 June 1913 by the trustees of the Barwick Charity.[38]

A boy scouts troop was formed at the College in 1909, the first members being sworn in by Robert Baden-Powell (see Fig. 18), and there was also a troop of girl guides. Known as 'the Raven Group', the scouts and guides used the reading room from 1977 to 1988, and then a room at the former corn mill.[39] Both scouts and guides still functioned in Kirkoswald in 2016 as the Second Eden Valley Cubs and Beavers and the First Kirkoswald and Langwathby Guide Unit.[40] The Kirkoswald branch of the Women's Institute was formed in 1920 with 42 members and continued monthly meetings at the Church Institute until 2002.[41] A youth club was started in 1960 at the Church Institute and continued to the late 1980s.[42] The Kirkoswald Mothers' Union was formed in 1957, and amalgamated with Lazonby and Great Salkeld in 1999.[43] Land for ten allotments was made available by Colonel Fetherstonhaugh in the 1920s on the west side of the road to

33   Inf. Timothy Fetherstonhaugh; *Cumberland & Westmorland Herald*, 9 Sept. 1950.
34   CAS (C), DS/94009/1, 13 Apr. 1863 (boys at the National School admitted to cricket club); Fetherstonhaugh, *Our Cumberland Village*, 80; minute books of cricket club from 1934 held by Neville Jackson.
35   Fetherstonhaugh, *Our Cumberland Village*, 80; inf. Neville Jackson and John Haugh.
36   *Kelly's Dir. Cumb.* (1897), 186.
37   Fetherstonhaugh, *Our Cumberland Village*, 79.
38   CAS (C), D/WAL/5.
39   Tiffin, *Memories of Kirkoswald*, 5; Fetherstonhaugh, *Our Cumberland Village*, 80.
40   Inf. Helen Armstrong and Fay Hoy.
41   CAS (C), DSO/259.
42   Inf. Neville Jackson.
43   CAS (C), PR 9/138 and 139.

Figure 18 *Photograph, taken in 1909 at the College, of the first meeting of the Kirkoswald boy scouts: in the centre is Robert Baden-Powell and next to him is Major (later Colonel) Timothy Fetherstonhaugh, author in 1925 of 'Our Cumberland Village': they had met in 1900 at Mafeking during the Boer War.*

Staffield, and a self-governing association of the allotment holders continued to function in 2016.[44]

Kirkoswald children entertained themselves with a wide range of games, many with singing and play acting, as well as 'Hare and Hounds' and 'English and Romans'.[45] Winter conditions allowed excellent tobogganing on Bellhouse Hill and on the main street, until the use of motor transport became general, and there was skating on Dolly Tarn at Highbankhill. The ruins of the castle were also a popular playground. Christmas, royal marriages and coronations were celebrated by parties for all the children either at the school or the College.[46]

Renwick maintained its own pattern of social activity. From 1857 to 1919 a Renwick Sons of Temperance group and a children's Band of Hope met regularly, the latter continuing until 1945.[47] There was a local musical tradition, and a choir which gave a

44   Inf. Timothy Fetherstonhaugh.
45   Revd J.J. Thornley, 'Children's games as played at the Parish of Kirkoswald', *CW2*, I, (1901), 268–79; Tiffin, *Memories of Kirkoswald*, 4–5.
46   Tiffin, *Memories of Kirkoswald*, 3–4.
47   CAS (C), DFCM 4/5/165 and 4/6/161/1; see also curate John Watson's remarks at DRC/Acc/A3966.

Figure 19 *Kirkoswald Church Institute (village hall), built 1910 on the western side of the market square in memory of James Mark Wood, lessee of the College.*

performance of Honegger's King David in 1937.[48] When the Board School replaced the National School in 1876, the 1838 building, owned by Queen's College, became surplus to requirements, and was renamed the reading room in 1879. It was for a time used as a place of resort for farm servants, and was furnished with a daily newspaper until 1950, after which it was closed for some years.[49] There was a Renwick Branch of the Women's Institute, from 1953 to 1974.[50] The celebrations for the Queen's Jubilee in 1977 resulted in a reopening of the reading room for meetings and community activities, with John Lishman (churchwarden 1977–2007) holding a tenancy from Queen's College; and the committee which organised the celebrations remained in place as a Sports Committee. Working in conjunction with the Anglican PCC and the Methodists, this committee oversaw growth in social and fundraising activities of many kinds. For some years there was a boules pitch and in 2005 a barn was fitted with a dance floor, and in that year a community choir was created to celebrate the centenary of the Methodist Chapel. The choir was still functioning in 2016.[51]

48   CAS (C), DX 1274/13, Parochial Magazine, Jun. 1945; concert handbill held by Rose Greenop.
49   Local inf.; also CAS (C), PR 72/7, dispute between vicar and Queen's College about the reading room as reported by *Cumberland & Westmorland Herald*, 17 Jan. 1914.
50   Inf. Anna Hartley, National Federation of Women's Institutes.
51   Local inf.

Education

The School at Highbankhill, Kirkoswald

A Kirkoswald schoolmaster called Arthur Bland was owed wages in 1613; and in 1631
Thomas Lowthian of Staffield was owed (by the parish) 36s 6d for the schoolmaster's
board.[52] Further schoolmasters in the middle decades of the 17th century were Thomas
Holmes (recorded 1650), Henry Bird and another Arthur Bland in 1672.[53] There is no
record of where these men taught.

John Rumney (d. 1738), curate of Renwick from 1680 and of Kirkoswald from
1685, was keeping a school by 1684, probably at Highbankhill where he lived, and well
placed for children from all three townships.[54] In 1723 Edmund Bird bequeathed £5, the
interest of which was to be paid to the schoolmaster at Highbankhill and his successors;[55]
and in 1738 Thomas Fetherstonhaugh bequeathed £4 for the use of the schoolmaster
at Highbankhill 'for teaching some poor parish boy or girl'.[56] Samuel Nicholson was
schoolmaster at Highbankhill from 1731 to 1743.[57]

In 1742 John Lowthian of Staffield Hall and Dumfries bequeathed £100 to be
expended in establishing a parish school and towards the schoolmaster's salary.
In advance of receiving these funds the parish of Kirkoswald built a new school at
Highbankhill, and invested the Lowthian legacy (and a separate sum of £20 of school
stock previously accumulated) to provide income towards the maintenance of the
schoolmaster, who was required to receive all the poor children of the parish, boys and
girls, and teach them reading at 1s. 6d. per quarter. The schoolmaster was to make his
own arrangements for teaching other subjects and other children (from Renwick for
example). Part of the legacy was later applied to the purchase of land and the remainder
invested, together with the parish poor stock, in the Eamont Bridge-Brough Turnpike
Trust.[58]

The endowed school at Highbankhill continued to function throughout the second
half of the 18th century and the first half of the 19th century.[59] In 1814 it was open
to all boys and girls belonging to the parish of Kirkoswald, the master being paid
quarter pence for all the scholars, but at a low rate for the poor in consideration of the
endowment; the average number of scholars was 36.[60] In 1818 there were two schools in
Kirkoswald parish: Highbankhill endowed school with 30 pupils, the master receiving

52   CAS (C), PROB/1615/WINVX210, inventory of Anthony Thompson, 1615; PROB/1631/WX65, will of
     Thomas Lowdyan, 1631; Fetherstonhaugh, A-19-1.
53   Baptism records; CAS (C), DRC 5/4 and 5/5.
54   Kirkoswald manor court 22 Oct. 1684; Staffield manor court 1710 ('Schoolhouse Beck').
55   CAS (C), PROB/1723/WINVX12, will and inventory of Edmund Bird, 1723.
56   Fetherstonhaugh, A-22-15.
57   CAS (C), DRC 5/22.
58   CAS (C), PROB/1742/W638, will of John Lowthian, 1742; PR 9/5 and PR 9/36; Jefferson, *Hist. & Antiq.*,
     297.
59   Baptisms 1772/7 and 1793/1805; CAS (C), DRC 5/81; Lysons, *Magna Britannia: Cumb.*, 130.
60   *Diocese of Carlisle*, 242.

£15 p.a. from the endowment and £18 in payment from the scholars; and a second, recently opened, day school also with 30 pupils.[61] In 1833 there were four day schools: Highbankhill endowed school (30 boys and 5 girls), and three private schools wholly supported by fees, two of which were small (together 4 boys, 26 girls), and the third (commenced in 1822) with 28 boys and 5 girls.[62]

Schools at Renwick

The school at Highbankhill would have served many Renwick children too, the distance being about two miles, until 1758 when a school house was built in Renwick.[63] There is no surviving record of where this school was and how it was managed, but it is probably the school referred to in 1814 as in receipt of a few shillings interest from a small endowment by Thomas Tallentire of Outhwaite.[64] Jonathan Grisedale was schoolmaster from 1797 to 1809, and may have continued to teach on his own account until his death in 1842.[65] The curate-teacher Thomas Robinson opened a school at Linghouse (near Scalehouses) in about 1790.[66]

In 1818 there was in Renwick a schoolhouse in which a mistress lived and taught 12 girls, and 2 schools, one with 27 pupils, and the other 45, 'taught by the minister' of whom 17 were Renwick children. This last was probably Linghouse, and one of the others the 1758 building.[67] By 1833 it seems that Linghouse had closed, and there were three daily schools: the 1758 school and two private schools which had commenced after 1818, at which some 67 boys and girls were educated, instruction being 'wholly at the expense of the parents'.[68] In 1838 the curate of Renwick, John Watson, petitioned for a new school building: the 1758 building was in decay and 'the population is chiefly agricultural, but many families are employed in coal and lime works, [and] are mostly so poor that the charge for schooling is often more than they are able or willing to spare.' A new school was built on waste ground near the church and, in 1840 when 34 girls and 30 boys attended, the school won the support of the National Society and (from 1847) Betton's Charity.[69] The 1838 National School in Renwick was replaced in 1876 by a larger Board (later Council) School at the southern edge of the village, with over 80 children being enrolled in the first year.[70] This school served the children of Renwick until 1987: there were 86 pupils in 1900, 40 in 1938 and 20 in 1956.[71]

61   *Educ. of Poor Digest.*
62   *Educ. Enq. Abstract.*
63   CAS (C), PR/72/7.
64   *Diocese of Carlisle*, 262; *Dir. Cumb.*, passim; probably an *inter vivos* gift of Thomas Tallentire (1696–1775).
65   CAS (C), DRC 5/72–80.
66   Kenneth Harper, 'John Atkinson, 1773–1857: Yeoman Schoolmaster', *CW2*, LXXXIII (1983), 158–60; *Diocese of Carlisle*, 264.
67   *Educ. of Poor Digest*: 'the minister' was Thomas Robinson.
68   *Educ. Enq. Abstract*; *Parson & White, Dir. Cumb.* (1929), 510–11 names Henry Moses as a schoolmaster.
69   CAS (C), PR/72/7.
70   CAS (C), DS/5941/6.
71   TNA, ED 161/226.

Figure 20 *Renwick reading room, built as a National School in 1838; owned by Queen's College Oxford, it is well used as a community meeting and activity room.*

Kirkoswald National (later Church of England) School

In 1855 the endowed school at Highbankhill educated 20 boys and 12 girls, and 23 boys and 27 girls attended two private day schools.[72] In 1856 the vicar of Kirkoswald, John Best, made a successful application to the Charity Commissioners on behalf of the trustees of the John Lowthian Trust for leave to sell the building at Highbankhill and apply the proceeds to the building of a new school closer to the centre of Kirkoswald.[73] A government grant was obtained towards building the new school intended for the instruction of the children of Kirkoswald's labouring poor (38 boys and 34 girls): the site was to be purchased freehold from William Richardson, timber merchant. In 1857 the National School in Sandhill, Kirkoswald was completed;[74] and in 2016, the building, not greatly altered, still housed the Kirkoswald Church of England Primary School, despite its frequently criticised location on a steep hill with limited space for a playground.[75]

The school was built at a cost of £608 for 125 children, in two rooms with living quarters for the head teacher. A grant of £298 was awarded, and over 50 persons

72 CAS (C), DCMA/11/15/2 (visitation, 1855).
73 TNA, ED 49/994.
74 TNA, ED 103/52/339; *P.O., Dir. Cumb.* (1858), 181; *Bulmer, Dir. Cumb.* (1901), 416; Fetherstonhaugh, *Our Cumberland Village*, 150.
75 The following account is drawn (unless otherwise stated) from CAS (C), DS/108/1/4, 185 (the school log books, access restricted); and also draws on William Roberts, *The Making of a School* (Kirkoswald & Renwick Local History Group, priv. printed, 2009).

and organisations contributed, notably Sir George Musgrave £50 and Timothy Fetherstonhaugh esq. and the Witherslack Trustees £20 each.[76] The first master, transferred from Highbankhill, was William Cowburn, assisted by a pupil teacher and monitors for the fourth and fifth classes. Enrolment was 70, both boys and girls, and attendance fluctuated whenever parents required the children (girls at any time, boys during turnip hoeing and harvest) to work at home. Absences also occurred during epidemics, in bad weather (since many children had to walk long distances to school), and, in January 1864, for vaccination against smallpox. Cowburn had difficulty in persuading parents to pay the quarter pence and 'coal money', and in 1863 was obliged to refuse entry to three underage children left at the school by their mothers. The children received basic instruction in reading, writing and arithmetic, but on request other subjects were taught; for example, in 1863, mechanical drawing to three boys destined for apprenticeship in Newcastle upon Tyne. Cowburn departed at Christmas 1863 to teach elsewhere and was succeeded by William Horner, newly out of training college at Chester, who was head teacher until 1881, assisted from 1877 (in which year average attendance was 113) by an assistant teacher and a pupil teacher. For several consecutive years school inspectors were critical of the quality of teaching in the school, and the grant to the school was reduced in each year from 1877 to 1880 inclusive. In 1881 the school managers resolved that 'the master should be seriously directed to the imperious necessity of great change by undeviating attention to fixed hours', and Horner resigned.[77] The headship changed four times in the following 16 years.

In 1897 Harvey Bradwell began 31 years as head teacher in Kirkoswald: he was highly regarded by the inspectors, and the school was noted for the excellent training given to young teachers. The children 'received a sound education in history, geography, general knowledge and nature study and even progressed to algebra and logs; there were inter-school competitions in essay writing which Kirkoswald frequently won'.[78] Brought under County Council control in 1903, the school was renamed Kirkoswald Church of England School in 1907: enrolment was over 90 and the usual attendance between 75 and 80. The management committee included four foundation managers (including the vicar who usually took the chair) and one manager, each appointed by the parish council and the County Education Committee. After 1947 there were two foundation managers and two managers each, appointed by the parish council and the County Education Committee.[79]

Bradwell retired in 1928. By 1939 the enrolment had fallen to about 60, but the arrival of 39 evacuee children from Newcastle upon Tyne made it necessary to find additional accommodation. Sidney Jopling, appointed in 1944, served as head teacher for 21 years. In 1948 Kirkoswald became a controlled school, and children over 14 were transferred to Lazonby: the following year children over 11 were likewise transferred and Kirkoswald then became a junior mixed and infant school with 56 pupils. A second assistant teacher was appointed in 1956, but with falling numbers she was soon removed. Jopling retired in 1965 and was succeeded by Valerie Lerew (the first female head teacher), with enrolment of about 40. The school was threatened with closure in the 1970s, strongly opposed by the community. In 1978, by which time enrolment had

76   CAS (C), PR 9/49.
77   CAS (C), PR 9/50, minutes of meetings of school managers.
78   Tiffin, *Memories of Kirkoswald*, 3.
79   CAS (C), DS/5940/1.

risen to 58, the schoolhouse was adapted to provide additional classrooms. In 1980 the threat of closure was lifted; the school was federated with Renwick school and received children from it when it closed in 1987. Kirkoswald Church of England Primary School became thenceforth the school for every primary-aged child in the enlarged parish of Kirkoswald. The playground was extended in 1989, and enrolment rose rapidly, to 73 in 1991, and 92 in 1992, at which time there were four full-time teachers. In 2016 there were 80 pupils.

Secondary education for Kirkoswald children was usually found at Penrith, with some Renwick children attending William Howard School at Brampton.

Welfare

Poor Relief Before 1834

Kirkoswald (until 1708 administered as one vestry and constablewick with Staffield) and Renwick each had overseers of the poor from 1642, if not earlier.[80] No overseers' accounts survive before 1715, but poor rates for the relief of the poor were doubtless being raised by purvey from at least 1642.[81] The long-running Kirkoswald *cause célèbre* of Robert and Ann Bowman is recorded in 11 petitions and counter-petitions to Quarter Sessions between 1693 and 1711.[82] The parish officials, under pressure from the increasing expense of administering poor relief, were at loggerheads with the magistrates in Quarter Sessions; and in 1706, according to the curate John Rumney, the overseer unjustly withheld 1s per week previously ordered by the magistrates; and in 1710 Ann Bowman, who was wearing the badge required by the 1697 Act, was (she claimed) refused the use of the ferry service over the river Eden and Mr Thomas Fetherstonhaugh threatened persons offering her shelter with reprisals. Whatever the truth of these allegations, it may be inferred from this episode, along with the Staffield petition in 1708 to be allowed to administer their own poor relief, and a series of manor court injunctions against the harbouring of incomers, that the expense of administering poor relief in the period 1690–1710 was causing severe discomfort.[83]

In Kirkoswald, in 1728/9, £10 16s. was collected and disbursed to nine individuals, four men and three women, at 1s. per week, and assistance was given with house rents and the cost of a pauper's funeral.[84] In 1749 an overseer was reprimanded for an 'extravagant' payment for attending a sick person, and overseers were instructed to tighten up the removal of lodgers without proper certificates. In 1753 an order was obtained from Quarter Sessions to erect a poor house at Kirkoswald which seems to have been built soon thereafter. Between 1754 and 1756 the governors were styled 'of

80   Parliamentary Arch., HL/PO/JO/10/1/82/113.
81   CAS (C), PR 9/5, churchwardens account book, 1641–4, 1707–8.
82   CAS (C), Q/11/1; for a full discussion of this case, see S. Hindle, 'Without the cry of any neighbours': a Cumbrian family and the poor law authorities' in H. Berry and E. Foyster (eds.), *The Family in Early Modern England* (Cambridge, 2007), 126–57; see also S. Hindle, *On the Parish? The Micro-Politics of Poor Relief in Rural England c.1550–1750* (Oxford, 2004), 51, 61, 80, 361–62, 414, 415, 439, 447.
83   Below, Local Govt.
84   CAS (C), PR 9/5 for 1715, 1729, 1730.

the stock and poor house': there was, however, no reduction in the number of persons receiving weekly support, and there is no further mention of a poor house.[85] In 1766 two pensioners, both widows with children, were receiving up to 3s per week.[86] In 1773 £5 12s. was spent on house rents and £4 17s. for clothing: in that year there were six pensioners in Low Quarter, four women and two men, and two of the women had children 'to be put out'.[87] In 1779 there were in the parish 16 pensioners, eight men and eight women. Sir Frederick Morton Eden, giving levels of expenditure from 1774 to 1794, recorded the highest annual spending (in 1791) as £140 5s. 2d. (over 300 purveys): he listed 19 persons seeking relief, including nine widows, seven bastard children, two old men, and a deserted wife with two children. In 1794 annual expenditure was about 4s. per head of population:[88] in 1801 it was 7s. 1d., in 1811 7s. 9d., in 1821 11s. 5d.; and in 1831 8s. 1d. In 1834 about 25 persons were receiving relief which was given 'according to absolute necessity'.[89]

In Staffield, responsible for its own poor relief from 1708, taxation and expenditure records survive from 1781.[90] In 1785 the unnamed overseer for High Quarter collected 48 purveys in three collections, yielding a total of £13 10s.; he disbursed *inter alia* money to buy shoes, shirts (and buttons), handkerchiefs, stockings and a hat for 'Betty Varey's son', and he recouped his expenses for 'binding two boys at Penrith.'[91] In 1815 James Armstrong of Scales, overseer for High Quarter, disbursed £36 11s. to five pensioners, all women. The standard payment was 3s. per week. Two recipients, Elizabeth Verrah and Rebecca Dixon, were assisted for 52 weeks, the former being a young married woman whose husband had either been enlisted or imprisoned (she also received house rent), and the latter an unmarried mother. Also in 1815, Armstrong disbursed £1 12s. to reimburse a payment to a substitute militia man. He remained in office for a further year, and continued payments to Verrah and Dixon, and two other women; he gave weekly support of 2s. 10d. to Christopher Elliott (cause of poverty unknown), and paid 5s. per week for 10 weeks for the board of Elizabeth Salkeld, another unmarried mother, with medical and christening fees.[92] In 1818 two men and two women were receiving house rent.[93] In 1832, the overseers John Little and John Lowthian (who farmed at Crindledyke in Low Quarter and Scales in High Quarter) stated that the expenditure on poor relief in 1831 was £163 or 12s. 3d. per head of population – high when compared with the Cumberland county average of 5s. 11d., the Kirkoswald and Renwick figures of 8s. 1d. and 7s. 4d., and the national average of 9s. 3d.. They also said 'there is no decision as to how much shall be collected, but the overseers collect again and again as often as money is wanted.'[94]

85   CAS (C), Q/8/2, p.14 (1753) and PR 9/5 for 1754–6.
86   CAS (C), PR 9/5.
87   CAS (C), PR 9/5.
88   Eden, *State of the Poor*, 83–7.
89   *Poor Law Com. 1st Rep.* image 1815, 2511, 3205, 3902, 4596.
90   CAS (C), PR 9/63, Staffield Rate Book.
91   CAS (C), PR 9/78; a purvey for High Quarter yielded 5s. 1d., for Low Quarter 3s. 11d.
92   CAS (C), PR 9/77.
93   CAS (C), PR 9/80.
94   *Poor Law Com. 1st Rep.* (image 1820): the figure for 1811 was £180, or 11s. 7d. per head.

In Renwick, where few poor law records survive, an assessment of 1*s*. in the £ was levied in 1807, yielding £20 7*s*., or 2*s*. per head of population.[95] Burial records for the 104 years from 1730 to 1833 recorded 19 persons as being in receipt of poor relief, nine men and ten women, mostly elderly. In 1832 Joseph Watson, assistant overseer, gave the following figures of expenditure with cost per head: 1803 £52 (5*s*. 2*d*.), 1813 £48 (3*s*. 5*d*.), 1821 £63 (3*s*. 5*d*.), 1831 £139 (7*s*. 4*d*.). He estimated the average labourer's wage as £35 p.a., and thought that 'the generality are always very poor'. Few owned the cottages in which they lived and only exceptionally would relief be given for rent.[96]

Poor Relief after 1834

After the formation of the Penrith Poor Law Union (PPLU), some residents of all three townships were admitted to Penrith Workhouse. In 1837, of 19 Kirkoswald claimants, 11 (eight women, three men) were receiving out-relief and eight were admitted to the workhouse (a mother with three children, three unaccompanied children and one man).[97] Two Kirkoswald men, aged 56 and 72, died at the workhouse in 1840 (as had two of the children admitted in 1837); three Staffield men died there between 1843 and 1851, aged 72, 87 and 76 (a former handloom weaver); and two Renwick women (widows aged 57 and 80) and one man (aged 51) died there between 1847 and 1851.[98] Recharges by the PPLU to all three townships in 1838 showed a significant reduction from the level of expenditure before 1836.[99] The previous practice of paying house rents to maintain the poor in their own homes was allowed to continue; and in all three townships over 70 per cent of the recharge was for out-relief, the balance being in-relief and administrative overheads.[100]

Parish Stocks and Charitable Bequests

The Kirkoswald poor stock, accumulated from bequests in wills and applied to both Kirkoswald and Staffield, amounted in 1641 to £31 3*s*. Loans were made annually at interest of 1*d*. for every shilling (about 8.5 per cent) to more than 50 individuals. The interest (some £2 10*s*.) was applied to many purposes, including wages for soldiers on training days, vermin bounties and increase of the stock. In the period 1642–4 there were distributions to the poor of up to 10*s* in each year; and in 1728×32 25*s*. in each year.[101] In 1761 the stock, which had by then risen to £62 10*s*., was invested (with school funds making a total of £100) at four per cent in the Eamont Bridge-Brough Turnpike Trust, and the interest was given to poor persons not receiving parish pay. After the dissolution

95   CAS (C), PR 9/118, thought to be a half-year assessment.
96   *Poor Law Com. 1st Rep.* (image 1818, 2514, 3208, 3905, 4599).
97   CAS (C), SPUP/1 (minutes of PPLU, 1837/41); later minutes, covering the economically bad years of the early 1840s, have not survived.
98   CAS (C), SPUP/130.
99   CAS (C), SPUP/130.
100 CAS (C), SPUP/1.
101 CAS (C), PR 9/5.

of the Turnpike Trust in 1881, £15 was recovered and applied to repaying debt on the township water supply.[102]

In 1742 John Lowthian of Staffield Hall and Dumfries, bequeathed the annual sum of £2 12s. to be applied to the purchase of a shilling's worth of bread to be distributed every week on Sunday to the poor people of Kirkoswald parish attending divine worship at St Oswald's church. In 1821 Richard Lowthian Ross, owner of Staffield Hall, was continuing to provide the funds, and distribution took place half after morning service and half after evening service. The terms of the bequest were being complied with in the 1880s and 1890s, and the last-known distribution of bread to the poor was made in January 1938.[103] Since 1945, the Lowthian bequest, still paid to the PCC in 2015, has been used for the purchase of altar bread.[104] In 1782 Richard Lowthian of Staffield Hall and Dumfries bequeathed £5 yearly to the poor of the parish: by 1897 the performance of this bequest had lapsed, and the funds had been lost.[105] Thomas Threlkeld of Caber (d. 1793), bequeathed £40 for the poor of Staffield, the interest of which was in 1855 given to 'poor persons not having weekly pay'.[106] William Parcival (d. 1746) of Renwick left £10 'to the poor of the parish', the interest divided at Christmas and Easter at the discretion of the curate and the churchwardens: in 1838 it was invested in consols.[107] There was no Renwick poor stock.[108]

A common lodging house in the Quebec area of Kirkoswald on land owned by the Fetherstonhaughs was recorded between 1851 and 1909;[109] probably first intended as the poor house, it stood close to the Raven Beck, just upstream from the corn mill. It was pulled down, and the site used for a pumping station, when the Penrith Rural District Council laid a new sewer to remove foul waste to a treatment plant at Lowfield in 1967.[110]

---

102 CAS (C), PR 9/35, vestry minutes 13 Apr. 1888; *Diocese of Carlisle*, 242, 365; Jefferson, *Hist. & Antiq.*, 297; see also Local Gvmt.

103 CAS (C), PROB/1742/W638, will of John Lowthian, 1742; PR 9/36; *5th Rep. Com. Char.*, 152–3; *Dir. Cumb.*, passim to 1938; PCC minutes (at Kirkoswald Vicarage) 4 Jan. 1938.

104 Inf. Canon David Fowler.

105 CAS (C), SPC/117/1/1, parish meeting 3 Apr. 1897; Jefferson, *Hist. & Antiq.*, 297; *Kelly's Dir. Cumb.* (1897), 185.

106 CAS (C), DCMA 11/15/2; *Dir. Cumb.* up to and including 1938.

107 CAS (C), PROB/1746/W127, will of William Parcival, 1746; *Kelly's Dir. C&W* (1938), 244.

108 Denton, *Perambulation*, 330.

109 Census, 1851–1901; *Porter, Dir. Cumb.* (1882); Fetherstonhaugh, B-15-7.

110 Tiffin, *Memories of Kirkoswald*, 2 ('an old dark house, where the sewage plant is now, used as a lodging house').

RELIGIOUS HISTORY

Origins and Parochial Organisation

THE DEDICATION TO THE NORTHUMBRIAN saint, Oswald, can be inferred from the name of the township. The existence of a spring under the west end of the church has been connected to Anglo-Saxon well worship.[1] An early medieval cross-arm, dated to the ninth or tenth century, was found during restoration work in the north wall of the church in 1879.[2] It therefore seems that there was an original Northumbrian foundation between the 8th and 10th centuries: if so, it was probably within the Northumbrian diocese of Hexham, the western boundary of which, it has been argued, lay on the river Eden.[3] Hexham's diocese ceased to operate before 900, and the situation is unclear thereafter: Durham, York and the forerunners of the bishops of Glasgow may have assisted with the provision of pastoral care. When the diocese of Carlisle was created in 1133, Kirkoswald

Figure 21 *St Oswald's Church, with Bell Tower Hill beyond and Easter cross of daffodils.*

1 See, e.g., Nicolson, *Misc. Acct.*, 116; however well worship may have had wider pagan origins.
2 Durham University, *Corpus of Anglo-Saxon Stone Sculpture*, http://www.ascorpus.ac.uk/catvol2.php (accessed 13 Feb. 2018).
3 C. Phythian-Adams, *Land of the Cumbrians: a study in British provincial origins, A.D. 400–1120* (Aldershot, 1996), 64, 69–70 and 102–3.

was, it seems safe to assume, transferred to it.[4] Renwick had become a separate parish by 1291.[5] The possibility that the ecclesiastical parish of Renwick may have been created out of that of Kirkoswald, perhaps in the 12th century, prevents any conclusion that this too was a pre-Conquest foundation.[6]

The two medieval parishes of Kirkoswald and Renwick remained unchanged until the 20th century. A Kirkoswald Deanery was created in 1926, and merged into the Penrith Deanery in 1969.[7] The benefices were reconfigured in 1941, when the northern and eastern parts of the parish of Kirkoswald were transferred to the parish of Renwick, and Renwick was united with Croglin; and in 1954 Kirkoswald was united with Renwick in a united benefice of Kirkoswald with Renwick (without Croglin). In 1976 Ainstable was added, and then detached in 2000, at which time Lazonby and Great Salkeld were added to make a united benefice of Kirkoswald, Renwick, Lazonby and Great Salkeld.[8] In 2012, the parish of Renwick was enlarged to include Croglin and became 'Renwick with Croglin'.[9]

Advowson

Kirkoswald

Kirkoswald church was rectorial until 1523, rectors having been recorded since the 13th century.[10] According to an agreement made in 1242, the advowson alternated between the lords of the Gernon and Multon moieties of the manor of Kirkoswald on the death of each rector until the two moieties were reunited in 1272.[11] After 1272 the patronage ran with the chief lordship of the manor: Thomas de Multon of Gilsland was recorded as patron in 1291 and John de Castre, knight, in 1323.[12] The Dacres, lords of the manor from 1329, were patrons of the parish from that time until the Reformation.

In 1523 Thomas, 2nd Baron Dacre of the North, created a collegiate church with an attached college for six priests, and at the same time endowed the college with the glebe and other lands and the tithes, yielding a total income in 1534 of more than £25 p.a.[13] The collegiate status was shared with the church at Dacre, and stipends were paid to the vicars of Kirkoswald and Dacre and to five chaplains. In 1550 the commission appointed to secure the forfeiture to the Crown of the possessions of the college were ordered by the Privy Council 'to suffer [the master and fellows] to reside and continue there as before

4   VCH, Cumb, II, 1 which states that Penrith was transferred in 1133.
5   Tax. Eccl. 129.1.
6   A.J.L. Winchester, Landscape and Society in Medieval Cumbria (Edinburgh, 1987), 24.
7   CAS (C), DRC 11/5/2; London Gaz., 13 Aug. 1926; with thanks to Canon David Fowler.
8   Orders in Council published in the London Gaz., 1 May 1941, 16 Apr. 1954, 11 Mar. 1976, 4 Dec. 1999 (at the vicarage, Kirkoswald).
9   CAS (C), PR 72/6; Orders in Council published in the London Gaz., 30 Mar. 1941, 16 Apr. 1954, 11 Mar. 1976, 4 Dec. 1999; draft scheme of the Church Commissioners, Feb. 2012.
10 Graham, 'Arthuret, Kirklinton and Kirkoswald', 52f.
11 TNA, CP 25/1/283/11, no.180; above Landownership.
12 Tax. Eccl. 320; Reg. John de Halton, II, 222–3.
13 Valor Eccl., 26.

… until such time as other order should be taken by his Majestie', and it seems that the college survived into and through the reign of Queen Mary.[14] Lord William died in 1563, and the last provost, Rowland Threlkeld, in 1565. The Crown, which had by this time acquired the patronage, retained it until 1877 when, by an exchange with West Ashby in Lincolnshire, it passed to the bishop of Carlisle.[15]

Renwick

The dedication of Renwick church to All Saints is recorded from the 18th century, perhaps preceded by St Benedict's.[16] Until about 1340, when it was appropriated to Hexham Priory, Renwick church (or chapel) was rectorial, an unnamed rector being referred to in 1335.[17] After the suppression of Hexham Priory, the advowson of the 'chapel or church of Ranwicke, called Ranwicke Chapel' was acquired by the Crown, which retained it when, in 1578, the possessions of the church were leased: however, at some unknown date before 1700, the patronage passed to the impropriators and may have been exercised alternately.[18] In 1739 James Westmorland became principal impropriator and patron.[19] In 1757 he sold the patronage to George Lawson, whose son William Lawson (1736–1819) was patron in 1814; and in 1849 William Lawson's grandson William de Lancy Lawson was described as 'the true and undoubted patron of the perpetual curacy of Renwick'.[20] In 1873 Joseph Nicholson purchased the patronage with the Lawson landholdings;[21] and after his death in 1895 it was held by William Salkeld to his death in 1935, and then by George Wilfred Armstrong, until the grouping with Croglin in 1941 introduced alternate exercise of the office.[22] After the union of the parishes of Kirkoswald and Renwick in 1954, the patronage of Renwick passed to the bishop of Carlisle.

Endowment

Kirkoswald

The church of Kirkoswald was recorded in 1291 valued at £48 1s. 5d.[23] When the diocese of Carlisle was taxed in 1318, Kirkoswald was recorded as being worth 100s.

14 *Acts of the Privy Council of England*, Vol 2, 1547–50, ed. John Roche Dasent (1890).
15 *London Gaz.*, 1 May 1877; with thanks to Canon David Fowler.
16 *N&B*, II, 435; T.H.B. Graham and W.G. Collingwood, 'Patron saints of the Diocese of Carlisle', *CW2*, XXV (1925) say 'medieval'; Prebendary Todd (1712) says St Benedict's (CAS (C), DX/1915/3); *Diocese of Carlisle* (1814) says 'St Benedict or All Saints'.
17 *Reg. John Kirkby*, I, pp. 39 (no. 235), 131 (no. 645).
18 Jefferson, *Hist. & Antiq.*, 107 makes this suggestion.
19 E. Hughes (ed.), *Fleming-Senhouse Papers* (Cumberland Rec. Ser. II, 1962), 108; CAS (C), DX 1705, box 1, package 5.
20 *Diocese of Carlisle*, 261; Lysons, *Magna Britannia: Cumb.*, 150; CAS (C), Q/R/J2/26; DCR/ 22/226 (indenture 19 Apr. 1849).
21 *Bulmer, Dir. Cumb.* (1884); CAS (C), D/BS, box 797.
22 CAS (C), PR/72/6.
23 *Tax. Eccl.*, 320.

and taxed for one tenth of that value.[24] The medieval church had extensive ancient glebe lands,[25] and with tithe and other revenues the church was well endowed. In 1523 these possessions passed to the newly created College, and in 1566, upon the suppression of the College, were forfeited to the Crown and leased to Thomas, 4th Baron Dacre, who died later that year.[26] Thereafter the Crown sold them, reserving the sum of £8 for a clergyman's stipend.[27] In 1586 Thomas Haughmond (Hammond), who had purchased the tithes from Thomas Skelton, expressed his intention to augment the stipend to £10 p.a., and to spend £10 on building a house for the incumbent.[28] It is possible that the policy of augmenting the stipend was continued by later patrons, including Sir Timothy Fetherstonhaugh, in whose time the parish was served by a graduate vicar, Robert Milburn.[29]

From 1725 Kirkoswald was able to support a resident vicar due to the purchase of glebe lands (houses and land at Highbankhill, Blunderfield and Lazonby) with the assistance of £200 from Queen Anne's Bounty and a matching amount raised from the parishioners: in 1731 the annual value of the benefice was £34 1s., and in 1777, after buying more glebe land at Penrith for £420, it had risen to £64.[30] John Fisher, vicar from 1774 to 1827, established a parsonage on the glebe land at Blunderfield, the first recorded place of residence of Kirkoswald incumbents.[31] In 1867 the parsonage at Blunderfield was pulled down and a new vicarage built, at a cost of £1,200, on an acre of land donated by Sir George Musgrave adjoining the road to Glassonby.[32] Funding included £400 from the Lord Chancellor, £200 by subscription, £200 from the Diocesan Society, £200 from the Church Commissioners and £200 from the incumbent John Best. In 1983 a house was purchased in Little Sandhill for temporary use as a vicarage for the enlarged benefice, and in 1985 a new site in Kirkoswald was purchased, and a vicarage built for £150,000, still in use in 2016.[33]

In 1703 Thomas Fetherstonhaugh (d. 1738) presented the church with books and 'a little press cupboard'.[34] Maintenance of the wall about Kirkoswald churchyard was traditionally the responsibility of the tenants of some of the larger farms in the parish, including Staffield: in 1768 eleven such tenants are recorded with the assigned lengths of

24   *Reg. John de Halton*, II, 188.
25   About 70 statute acres – above Landownership, the College Estate.
26   *Cal. Pat.* Eliz I, vol.3, no. 2439.
27   Fetherstonhaugh, A-20-1.
28   CAS (C), DSEN/14/3/1/102.
29   See below, *Religious Life*.
30   CAS (C), DRC 22/167, terriers of 1731, 1749 and 1777; by 1938 the value of the living had risen to £330, see *Kelly's Dir. C&W* (1938), 195.
31   *Diocese of Carlisle*, 154.
32   CAS (C), DRC 22/167, terrier of 1867.
33   Inf. Canon David Fowler.
34   CAS (C), PR 9/5, churchwardens account book, 1704–5. In his will of 1738, Thomas Fetherstonhaugh also bequeathed money for the repair of pews and for building a house for the vicar (Fetherstonhaugh, A-22-15).

wall and their proprietorial marks; and an additional sum to complete the task of repair was raised by the purvey.[35] In 1859 a hearse was acquired by public subscription.[36]

Renwick

In 1291, the church or chapel was valued at £9 11s. 4d.[37] In 1318, however, its income was reckoned insufficient to cover the ordinary requirements of the church and it was therefore exempt from taxation, perhaps because of damage caused by the Scots.[38] The ancient glebe lands amounted to about 35 a. (15 ha); and in 1479 there was a priest-house.[39] After the suppression of Hexham Priory, the possessions of the church (excepting the bells and the lead) were leased by the Crown to Thomas Owen for 13s. 4d. p.a., reserving the sum of £4 p.a. for a curate's stipend: the glebe land and tithes were thereafter in the hands of lay impropriators (principally Miles Gosling of Renwick).[40] Between 1614 and 1616, Thomas Gosling, son of Miles, sold the tithes of wool and lamb to Henry Fetherstonhaugh, and, separately to other parties, the tithes of corn and hay and the glebe land. In 1639 the parishioners commenced a chancery action against Sir Timothy Fetherstonhaugh and the other impropriators, seeking an order that they should pay more towards the curate's stipend. It was said that the stipend of the curate William Atkinson, which was 20 marks per year (£13 6s. 8d.), was insufficient to secure the services of a sufficiently learned minister. The defence pleaded lawful acquisition of the tithes and glebe land, and contended that there were other sources of income available to the curate, including the tithes of animals (other than lambs) and poultry. The result of the case is not known, perhaps it never came to trial.[41]

The £4 stipend for the curate of Renwick was augmented from lands at Hunsonby and Ainstable purchased in the 1720s with £600 from Queen Anne's Bounty (and a further £200 from the countess dowager Gower); in 1749 moduses were payable in lieu of tithes for corn hemp and linen from the hamlets of Scalehouses and Outhwaite, and from the parish at large for hay; and small fees were payable for rites of passage, and a smoke penny at Easter.[42] The value of the living was £13 in 1749; £40 in 1777; £70 in 1814; £90 in 1847; and £125 in 1884.[43] A vicarage was built in the 1870s by public subscription on land (thought to be the site of the medieval priest-house) donated by the patron William de Lancy Lawson.[44] In 1917–19 £850 was raised from grants and local fundraising, and the income from these funds, from a legacy and the proceeds of sale of the land at

35 CAS (C), PR 9/5, churchwarden's account book, 1768; some proprietorial marks could still be seen in 2016.
36 CAS (C), DCC/Acc/3966.
37 *Tax. Eccl.* 129.1.
38 *Reg. John de Halton*, II, 188.
39 *Priory of Hexham*, II, 12.
40 *Cal. Pat. Eliz.* I, vol. 7, no. 3251.
41 TNA, C 2/ChasI/R51/19 (1639); Fetherstonhaugh A-20-5 (1614).
42 CAS (C), DRC 22/226, terriers of 1749 and 1777.
43 CAS (C), DRC 22/226 and *Diocese of Carlisle*, 262, 264; *Mannix & Whellan, Dir. Cumb.* (1847), 303–4; *Bulmer, Dir. East Cumb.* (1884).
44 *Slater, Dir. Cumb.* (1884), 120–1; CAC (C), DRC 22/226.

Hunsonby and Ainstable, allowed the vicar's annual stipend to be raised to £250 in 1920, and to £300 in 1927.[45]

Two medieval church bells, believed to have been originally made for and installed at Renwick, have been dated to about 1400:[46] the larger bell, inscribed with an alphabet of 23 letters in Lombardic capitals and replaced in 1893, was transferred to Carlisle Cathedral Treasury in 2012.

Religious Life

Direct evidence of religious life in the Middle Ages is limited. The earliest-named rector of Kirkoswald was a certain Martin, recorded in 1242 and 1246.[47] Walter Langton, from 1296 bishop of Coventry and Lichfield, resigned as rector in 1292/3.[48] A royal officer, he was a noted pluralist and undoubtedly an absentee.[49] Nicholas de Luvetot was presented in his place, and held the benefice in 1308; two further presentations to the living were made by 1316.[50] The churches of both Renwick and Kirkoswald were noted as destroyed following hostilities from the Scots in 1302;[51] but in 1305 Bishop John de Halton was able to perform diocesan business at Kirkoswald.[52] In 1335 the rector of Renwick was presented for failure to profer canonical obedience to the bishop.[53]

Until c.1565, the dominance in eastern Cumberland of the Barons Dacre of the North, a staunchly Roman Catholic family, no doubt encouraged continued adherence to Rome, but after their departure there is no evidence that Catholicism remained entrenched in Kirkoswald for long. During the second half of the 17th century, non-conformity took a firm hold in Kirkoswald, where a gathered church of protestant dissenters attracted rapidly growing support from 1653; and, by 1851, four of the six main places of worship in Kirkoswald and Renwick were nonconformist.

Kirkoswald

In 1559 John Scales, who had been listed in 1534 as one of six priests receiving a stipend from the College, was recorded as vicar.[54] After Scales' death in 1566, James Shepherd was instituted to the vicarage of Kirkoswald by right of the queen: Shepherd served first as curate and later as vicar, and died in 1577.[55] His successor, Thomas Carter, who served as curate until 1585 and later as vicar, began the registration of births, deaths and

45   Vestry minute book at Kirkoswald Vicarage.
46   Revd H. Whitehead, 'Church bells in Leath Ward, no. 5', CW1, XIV (1896), 259f.
47   Graham, 'Arthuret, Kirklinton and Kirkoswald', 52f.
48   Reg. John de Halton, I, 3.
49   ODNB, s.v. Langton, Walter (d. 1321), administrator and bishop of Coventry and Lichfield (accessed 19 Jun. 2018).
50   Reg. John de Halton, I, 3–4, 297; II, 127.
51   Reg. John de Halton, I, 196.
52   Reg. John de Halton, I, 241–6, II, 24–7.
53   Reg. John Kirkby I, 39–40, (nos 235–6).
54   Valor. Eccl., 26; C.J. Kitching (ed.), The Royal Visitation of 1559 (Surtees Soc., vol. 187, 1972), 104.
55   CAS (C), DRC 1/3/21 (Bishop Best's register).

marriages at Kirkoswald in April 1577.[56] Both Shepherd and Carter used the simplest terminology in composing wills, disclosing neither continued adherence to Rome, nor leanings towards Puritanism.[57] Carter died in 1601 and was succeeded by John Allam who was vicar by 1606 and still the incumbent in 1620.[58]

Between 1620 and 1642 no Kirkoswald incumbent was recorded in diocesan records, but somebody was conducting baptisms, marriages and burials, and recording them, for all years between 1620 and 1642.[59] Arthur Bland, clerk, was recorded as a teacher in Kirkoswald between 1620 and 1633, and William Wilson, clerk, was raising a family in Kirkoswald between 1636 and 1640; either or both may have held the cure of St Oswald's.[60] Robert Milburn, a graduate, was vicar from March 1642 until his death in 1651: it seems likely that he, and most of his congregation, would in doctrinal matters have followed the lead of Sir Timothy Fetherstonhaugh and the policy of King Charles.[61]

After the deaths of Sir Timothy Fetherstonhaugh and Robert Milburn in 1651–2, religious life in the parish of Kirkoswald was profoundly changed by the emergence of an Independent congregation of protestant dissenters, and for some 30 years the authority of the Church of England in the parish of Kirkoswald was seriously undermined (see Nonconformity). Milburn was not replaced by a resident incumbent for more than 30 years. From 1668 George Yates rector of Croglin, Thomas Robinson curate of Addingham, and George Sanderson (Yates' successor at Croglin) were in turn assigned to the cure of Kirkoswald, but struggled to perform the task.[62] The church register was maintained in good order until March 1659, but from 1660 to 1685 all entries seem to be backdated and haphazard.[63] Somebody, however, was able to submit bishop's transcripts for some of those years, and in 1667, 1673 and 1678 they were signed by Sanderson. The Independents appear to have had control of St Oswald's Church from 1653 and, despite the enactments of the Clarendon Code and the efforts of the magistrates to enforce them, did not altogether relinquish it until about 1680.

In 1685 John Rumney, the curate of Renwick, was appointed to the cure of Kirkoswald as well. He lived at Highbankhill, half way between the two. He served as curate of Kirkoswald from 1685 to 1712, and as vicar from 1725 to his death in 1738.[64] Rumney was succeeded in 1738 by John Mandeville; and he in turn in 1761 by Charles Smalwood, the husband of Joyce Fetherstonhaugh of the College, Kirkoswald, whose son Charles Smalwood inherited the College estate in 1797 (above, Landownership).

---

56 CAS (C), PR 9/1, the first parish register, which was used until 1659.

57 CAS (C), PROB series, Kirkoswald wills from 1566 to 1601.

58 CAS (C), DRC 5/1; PROB/1620/WINVX18, will of William Bowman, 1620.

59 CAS (C), PR 9/1.

60 Nightingale, *Ejected of 1662*, 332; for Bland see also Fetherstonhaugh, A-19-1 (1615, 1620) and CAS (C), PROB/1634/WX20, will of Thomas Bowman, 1634.

61 HL/PO/JO/10/1/82/113; Milburn was buried at Kirkoswald 28 Feb 1651; Nightingale, *Ejected of 1662*, 333.

62 CAS (C), DRC 5/2, DRC 5/3, DRC 5/4, recorded as either 'lector' or 'curate'; Yates and Sanderson verified 22 Kirkoswald inventories from 1669 to 1685.

63 CAS (C), PR 9/1 and PR 9/2, the two earliest surviving church registers.

64 CAS (C), DRC 5/5 and 5/6, call rolls of clergy in Cumberland Deanery; between 1712 and 1725 the curates were James Wannup, William Milner (DRC 5/6) and Rumney himself in 1724 (bishop's transcript); for Rumney as a teacher, above, Social History.

St Oswald's church was well supported in Victorian times. In 1864 the vicar John Best held morning and afternoon services with sermons and a cottage lecture once a week, and there were 60 communicants, average attendance 30, collections for Pastoral Aid Society and Church Missionary Society, a Sunday school for children up to age 14, and monthly lectures for adults in the reading room and library. In 1872 John Best described St Oswald's as 'one of the best attended country churches in the diocese'.[65] Canon John Thornley (see Fig. 22) started a church magazine in 1895.[66]

Renwick

Jeffrey Gosling, perpetual curate of Renwick from 1589, supplemented his income by holding a customary farming tenement at Outhwaite.[67] After his death in 1616, there is no record of any further curate of Renwick until 1639, when one William Atkinson held the cure. George Mires, a Parliamentary appointment in 1649, served as resident perpetual curate to his death in 1668.[68] It seems likely that doctrinally Mires would

LATE CANON THORNLEY
KIRKOSWALD VICARAGE

Figure 22 *Postcard (1906) depicting Kirkoswald Vicarage and the late Canon John Thornley who published scholarly work on the early Kirkoswald church registers, field names and children's games.*

---

65   CAS (C), DCC/Acc/3966.
66   CAS (C), DX 1076/1.
67   QC, 5A-13; CAS (C), DRC 5/1 (1606); PROB/1589/WINVX171, will of Miles Westmorland, 1589; PROB/1616/WINVX68, will of Jeffrey Gosling, 1616.
68   CAS (C), DRC 5/2; PROB/1668/WX86, will of George Mires, 1668; Mires was overlooked by Nightingale.

have been in sympathy with the Kirkoswald Independents, and Renwick families seem to have remained loyal to his ministry. In 1662 Mires (who must have done what was necessary to avoid ejection) wrote, in the annual return to the bishop, 'there are none but are ready to come to divine service'.[69] When Mires died in 1668, he was replaced by Robert Nelson,[70] and after him in 1675 by George Dacre vicar of Ainstable.[71] In 1680 John Rumney was appointed curate of Renwick and in 1685 he was also appointed to Kirkoswald, where he drew up long lists of dissenters – but made no equivalent presentments for Renwick and had nothing to report there from between 1699 and 1710.[72] For many decades after Rumney's death in 1737, Renwick was served by the incumbents of other parishes, for example William Wilkinson, vicar of Lazonby, who served Renwick from 1741 to 1762. In 1747 the people of Renwick complained about having service only once every three weeks.[73]

   In 1807 Renwick again acquired a resident clergyman, Thomas Robinson, who lived at Scalehouses and also served neighbouring Croglin. Robinson, like Rumney before him, was both clergyman and teacher, and served Renwick as curate until his death in 1831. He was succeeded by John Watson who lived at Croglin and was curate of Renwick for 34 years, during which he oversaw both the establishment of a National School in 1838 (see Social History) and the rebuilding of the church in 1845–6. The average attendance at church in 1858, when services were held every Sunday either in the morning or the afternoon, was 40 and 75 respectively; communion was infrequent (three or four times a year) and the number of communicants usually ten. In 1858, John Watson gave charity sermons for 'Indian sufferers', SPCK and the Bible Society. After Watson's death in 1866, he was replaced by Michael Valentine Kennedy who, like most of his successors but not his predecessors, was a graduate.[74] In 1867 the living was enlarged to a vicarage, with Kennedy as first vicar. In 1900 it was said that 'scarcely 20 per cent' of the population attended the parish church. At that time communion was held monthly, with eight communicants.[75]

Nonconformity

The Kirkoswald Independents

The first steps in the creation of an Independent congregation on the east side of the river Eden were taken at Melmerby in 1653, and in the same year there was a proposal to appoint a pastor for the church gathered 'in and about Kirkoswald'.[76] John Davis, a noted non-conformist divine, who was 'sent by Cromwell to supply places in the north',

69   CAS (C), DRC 6/122.
70   CAS (C), DRC 5/3, 114.
71   CAS (C), DRC 5/4, 127.
72   CAS (C), DRC 6/122.
73   CAS (C), DMH 10/3/5, p. 89.
74   Crockford's Clerical Dir. (1884).
75   CAS (C), DRC/Acc/A3966.
76   TNA, RG 4/566, 4-6, a copy of the original church covenant made by Caleb Threlkeld from a paper given to him by Mrs Rebecca Nicholson, widow of George Nicholson; Cockermouth, 8–9.

purchased a manorial tenement in Kirkoswald in 1656, married there in 1657 and moved on to Northumberland in 1659.[77] He was succeeded by George Nicholson (1636–97), who was born in Kirkoswald, attended Magdalene College Oxford, 'went down into Cumberland a little before the Bartholomew Act took place' (1661 or 1662) and died

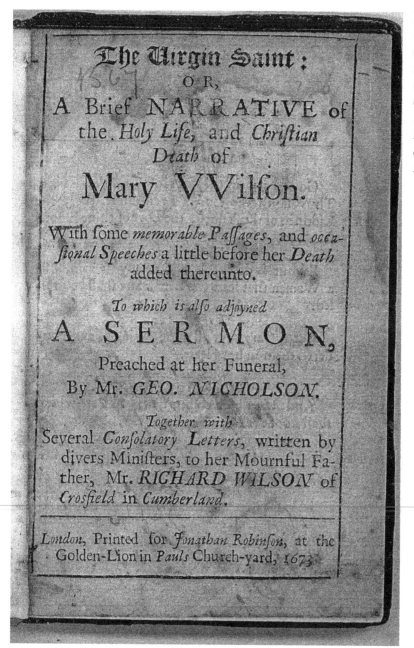

Figure 23 'The Virgin Saint': frontispiece of a book, published in London in 1673, to mark the passing of Mary Wilson, 19-year-old daughter of Richard Wilson, elder of the Huddlesceugh Independent church.

77   Cockermouth, 16n; CAS (C), DMUS/1/6/1/3, Kirkoswald Manor Court Oct. 1659; the quotation is from Nightingale, *Ejected of 1662*, 334; A.G. Matthews (ed.), *Calamy Revised*, 366.

Figure 24 *Parkhead (Huddlesceugh) Independent Chapel, built 1711, now a private house.*

at Kirkoswald in 1697 after 35 years of ministry.[78] Prominent among those supporting Nicholson in the 1670s and 1680s was Richard Wilson of Crossfield (Staffield), who was recorded as an elder of the Independent church at Kirkoswald in 1673 and 1678, and whose daughter Mary Wilson, who died aged 19 in 1672, was remembered as 'the Virgin Saint' (see Fig. 23).[79] In 1700 Nicholson's successor, Caleb Threlkeld, recorded 191 names of persons worshipping in the Independent church (not all resident in Kirkoswald).[80]

The strength of the Independents is shown by an order of Bishop Edward Rainbow of Carlisle dated 10 April 1673. George Towry of Croglin Hall, a recent arrival in the parish, had in 1663 become impropriator by acquisition of the right to receive tithes, and had been assigned a pew in the church. It was claimed that:

> some of the parish have abetted & animated their servants or children to intrude forcibly into the said pew and to molest & keep out George Towry & his family from sitting there and particularly that a rude fellow was permitted to threaten Mr Burton a neighbouring minister then officiating ... with many reproachful words ..., and [they] have also discouraged divers ministers who have freely offered ... to preach in that church which hath been so long destitute of a minister.[81]

The order, marked 'for Mr George Sanderson the minister of Kirkoswald and any other minister who officiates in the church of Kirkoswald', also demanded the return of the church key. The lack of resident clergy, hostility in the local community and dissenters' purloining of the church key were not the only problems: there were several years in

78   A.G. Matthews (ed.), *Calamy Revised*, 366 (the Bartholomew Act was the Act of Uniformity 1662); for Nicholson's ministry see Nightingale, *Ejected of 1662*, 337–41.
79   *Cockermouth*, 50, 70; Carlisle Central Library, Jackson Collection, *The Virgin Saint*; Nicolson, *Misc. Acct.*, 118 (memorial to Mary Wilson in Kirkoswald church).
80   TNA, RG 4/566, p. 3.
81   CAS (C), DSEN/14/3/1/102.

which no churchwardens were appointed, and other years in which appointees refused to serve.[82]

The magistrates punished the Independents for offending against the Clarendon Code, and in 1670 compelled them to meet in groups of four.[83] It seems that in about 1680 an agreement was reached under which the Independents acquired land at Huddlesceugh which they could use as a meeting place without attracting the hostile attention of the magistrates.[84] George Nicholson is recorded as owning a barn at Huddlesceugh in 1684, and it seems likely this was used for their worship for the next 30 years.[85]

George Nicholson died in 1697, and in 1700 the Independents appointed another local man, Caleb Threlkeld (1676–1728), to succeed him. From 1700 Threlkeld kept a record of baptisms, and in 1711 he oversaw the building of a chapel, later known as Parkhead Chapel, on the site of the previous meeting place (see Fig. 24).[86] The endowment included a manse, barn, an adjacent field, burying ground and Hall's Close.[87] Parkhead Chapel was well supported by the people of Kirkoswald and Staffield (as well as more distant families), but only two Renwick families (Hilton and Sowerby) baptised their children at Parkhead between 1700 and 1750.[88]

It seems that ill feeling between the Kirkoswald congregations resurfaced in 1712. Soon after Parkhead Chapel had been built, Threlkeld was accused in Quarter Sessions of threatening James Tolson, a blind member of his congregation, with physical violence: Threlkeld was bound over to keep the peace, resigned and moved to Dublin. At about the same time John Rumney resigned his curacies of Kirkoswald and Renwick and took up a teaching post in neighbouring Addingham. There is nothing on record to relate these two events, but the coincidence is striking.[89]

The Independents were without a resident minister until 1733, when Adam Dean began more than half a century of ministry at Parkhead Chapel.[90] Before 1760 the Independents used the parish churchyard, but thereafter buried their dead at Parkhead.

In the 19th century the Independents continued to prosper. Additional chapels were built in Gamblesby in 1824 and in Back Lane, Kirkoswald before 1851.[91] All three chapels were served by William Gibson, from 1839 to 1847, and Joseph Redmayne from 1847 to 1860. In 1851 Redmayne wrote 'at Kirkoswald we have held open communion with such recognised members of the Wesleyan Society as choose to join us, and would here

---

82   CAS (C), PR 9/5, appointments of village officers 1667/1670; CAS (C), DRC 5/4.
83   *Cockermouth*, 37.
84   There is no surviving record of an agreement; CAS (C), DSEN/14/3/1/102 is an undated letter from 14 tithe payers, nine of whom were dissenters, saying 'Mr Sanderson will have his £8'.
85   CAS (C), DMUS/1/6/1/3 (Kirkoswald manor court 22 Oct. 1684); the author thanks David Wykes, director of the Williams Library, Euston, for the suggestion that a barn was used for worship.
86   TNA, RG 4/566, p. 3.
87   CAS (C), DFCCL 13/12A; Hall's Close, 6 acres, was purchased with £20 bequeathed before 1712 by John Hall of Headsnook for the support of a minister at Huddlesceugh: TNA, RG 4/566, p. 8.
88   TNA, RG 4/566, p. 30.
89   CAS (C), Q/11, 1712, doc 15; TNA, RG 4/566, p. 8; Threlkeld died in Dublin in 1728 and is remembered for his published work on botany: *ODNB*, s.v., Threlkeld, Caleb (1676–1728), physician and botanist (accessed 19 Jun. 2018).
90   TNA, RG 4/566, pp. 20–1.
91   TNA, HO 129/565; TNA, RG 4/688.

express a hope that such may long continue to be the case'.[92] A Sunday school with four teachers and 16 scholars was commenced in 1868.[93] The three chapels belonged to the Cumberland Congregational Union from 1871.[94] The highest combined attendance at Kirkoswald and Parkhead chapels, in 1889, was 71, and there were a bible class and mutual improvement societies for young men and women.[95] Three bequests to Parkhead chapel were recorded in the 1880s and 1890s.[96]

In 1891 the last full-time resident minister at Parkhead, Robert Batey, was appointed to serve the chapels at Parkhead, Kirkoswald and Gamblesby at a salary of £66 p.a. plus a grant of £20 received from the Congregational Union.[97] Parkhead chapel was registered for the solemnisation of marriages in 1901.[98]

Methodism

The arrival of Methodism would have an impact on religious life in Kirkoswald and Renwick at least as great as that of the Independent movement in the 1650s. Before 1800 Parkhead chapel was the only purpose-built place of dissenting worship in Kirkoswald and Renwick. When John Wesley preached at Gamblesby in 1780, the Watsons (stonemasons of Renwick, and themselves influential) were there to hear him, and, together with the farming family of Greenop, became prime movers in establishing Renwick Methodist Chapel.[99] Methodist worship was certified in a private house at Scalehouses, Renwick, in 1813.[100] In 1818 a cottage-like chapel was built on land acquired by Joseph Lowthian under the Renwick Enclosure Award and donated by him to newly appointed Trustees.[101]

The number of Methodists in Renwick was described as 'a few' in 1825.[102] The Wesleyans established a Sunday school in 1817;[103] and added a schoolroom to their chapel in 1863.[104] In 1851 attendance at Renwick Wesleyan chapel was 75 and, together with a group of 38 primitive Methodists who attended services in a private house, Methodists in Renwick outnumbered Anglicans by almost three to one.[105] It seems, however, that Methodists continued to attend regularly at Anglican services and to use the church for rites of passage for most of the 19th century. Renwick Wesleyan Chapel was rebuilt (the schoolroom being retained) in 1905 by Thomas Henry Dryden (1856–

---

92   CAS (C), DFCCL 13/11, p. 10.
93   CAS (C), L13/5/11.
94   CAS (C), DFCCL 13/1, reports of the Cumberland Congregational Union.
95   Ibid.
96   CAS (C), DFCCL 13/43.
97   CAS (C), DFCCL/13/12A
98   *London Gaz.*, 8 Feb. 1901.
99   J. Platt, 'Thomas Watson, peasant-poet', *Northern History*, XLIX (2012), 323; *Cumberland and Westmorland Advertiser*, 1 Jul. 1884, p. 6.
100 Certificate of Methodist Worship 1813 (in Renwick Methodist schoolroom).
101 Foundation deed 1818 at Kirkoswald Manse.
102 *Diocese of Carlisle*, 263.
103 CAS (C), DFCM 4/5/160; *Parson & White Dir. C&W* (1829), 510.
104 *Bulmer, Dir. Cumb.* (1884), 686.
105 TNA, HO 129/565.

1941), a local builder.[106] A compact and commodious building, with seating for 150 and a good organ, it is described as having 'porch mock-fortified in a half-hearted way, with battlements and a clock on a backless tower behind it'.[107]

A Methodist chapel was built in Sandhill, Kirkoswald in 1821.[108] In 1851 there were in the township of Kirkoswald five places of worship, Anglican, Methodist, and three Independent (including a private house at Busk which held a small monthly gathering). The Methodists were enjoying rapid growth, their congregation of 130 outnumbering the independents, and non-conformist congregations together outnumbered the Anglicans by about three to one.[109] In 1871 Kirkoswald Methodist Chapel was rebuilt, at a cost of £1,000, on land donated by Sir George Musgrave on the right-hand side of the road to Staffield, and in 1874 a manse was built opposite to it.[110] The new chapel held 242 sittings[111] and was registered for the solemnisation of marriages in 1875.[112] The first quarterly meeting of the newly formed Kirkoswald circuit was held at Kirkoswald on 27 September 1871.[113] In 1878 Canon John Ransom, vicar of Kirkoswald, wrote 'Wesleyanism has a strong hold on the people here & there is a small body of Independents, neither strongly antagonistic to the church system'.[114] In 1904 the Methodist Sunday school was attended by 26 children.[115]

Religious Life in Kirkoswald and Renwick after 1918

Before 1914 it was not unusual for Kirkoswald residents to attend divine service at St Oswald's and the two non-conformist chapels on the same Sunday,[116] but after 1918 all denominations suffered declining attendance. The Independent churches failed to survive: in 1927 the Cumberland District Committee of the Congregational Union was told that 'church life is almost non-existent in [Parkhead] Chapel and its branches at Kirkoswald and Gamblesby', and a decision was made not to replace Robert Batey:[117] all activity ceased thereafter at Kirkoswald Chapel, and authority to sell it was given by the Charity Commissioners in 1938.[118] In 2016 it was used for storage. Parkhead Chapel was sold in 1975 and was a private house in 2016.[119]

---

106 *Mid Cumberland and North Westmorland Herald*, 15 Jul. 1905.

107 Hyde & Pevsner, *Cumbria*, 588.

108 1821 date stone on building; *Parson & White, Dir C&W* (1829), 491.

109 TNA, HO 129/565; CAS (C), DFCM 4/1/75.

110 Trust deed of 6 Dec. 1870 in possession of Superintendent Minister of the circuit; for the manse, Fetherstonhaugh, A-6-14 and CAS (C), DFCM 4/1/17.

111 CAS (C) DFCM 4/1/4.

112 *London Gaz.*, 5 Jan. 1875.

113 CAS (C), DFCM 4/1/1; the circuit included chapels at Gamblesby, Hunsonby, Ainstable, Skirwith, Renwick, Langwathby, Glassonby, Lazonby, Salkeld Dykes, Ousby and Temple Sowerby.

114 CAS (C), DCC/Acc/3966.

115 *London Gaz.*, 5 Jan. 1875; CAS (C), DFCM 4/1/76.

116 Oral evidence of Florence Tiffin (b 1908), taken by Ruth Lee (who holds it) in 1993.

117 CAS (C), DFCCL 13/5, 181.

118 CAS (C), DFCCL 13/12A and 13/43.

119 *Cumberland & Westmorland Herald*, 1 Mar. 1975.

The Anglican churches and the Methodist chapels in both Kirkoswald and Renwick also experienced falling congregations but continued to function into the 21st century. In 1939 the Kirkoswald Anglicans organised the knitting of blankets by schoolgirls for Polish refugees.[120] The vicar John Bailey was ambitious to increase and improve the church choir and gave regular lectures at the Church Institute about missionary work. In August 1945 it was recorded that 'there has lately been a falling off of attendance in [St Oswald's] church'; and in 1946 Sir Richard and Lady Denman organised a meeting at Staffield Hall 'to promote the drawing together of Christian bodies', a forerunner of the 2015 initiative to promote closer relations between Anglicans and Methodists (see below).[121]

In 1945 the Kirkoswald Methodists raised funds for the rebuilding of bombed churches.[122] In 1950 they extended their chapel to create a kitchen; and in the 1980s their former schoolroom was made into a chapel and furnished with the communion rail and pulpit from the recently closed Ousby Chapel. At the same time the pews were removed in the main chapel and there was a service of rededication in 1997.[123] The average attendance in 2014 was 25.[124] In 2016 the chapel was used, in addition to worship, for a variety of community activities including school productions, a choir and meetings of the guides.[125]

Falling attendance at All Saints Church, Renwick was noted in 1963, and the annual church fete began from that time, one of a number of fundraising schemes continued into the 21st century.[126] In 2016, after Renwick parish had been extended to include Croglin, average attendance was about 15, communion being held three times a month.

The Renwick Methodists, with an enduring basis of support from the Greenop family and other families with a long history of involvement, continued to run a Sunday school until the 1980s (the Anglicans having discontinued theirs in the 1960s). In 2005 they celebrated the centenary of the rebuilding of their chapel with an exhibition and a concert.[127] Both Anglicans and Methodists supported measures for closer collaboration, and in 2016 there was a tradition of holding joint services five times a year. Fundraising activities (for example a weekly coffee morning at the Methodist schoolroom, and in summer time afternoon tea at the reading room organised by Anglicans) were coordinated and mutually supported. Determined fundraising and strong public support for the resulting community activity ensured that the small village of Renwick still had two functioning places of worship in 2016.

In December 2015 a meeting was convened in Kirkoswald by Bishop James Newcome of Carlisle to discuss with both Anglicans and Methodists their developing collaboration. From this has developed a plan for broader cooperation, involving adjoining Anglican

120 CAS (C), DX 1274/7.
121 CAS (C), DX1274/13.
122 CAS (C), DFCM 4/1/4.
123 Planning approval 1950, in possession of Superintendent Minister; *Wesley Historical Society Cumbria*, Autumn 1986, 2 (with thanks to Ralph Wilkinson); inf. Helen Armstrong.
124 The Methodist Church, *Statistics for Mission* (2014).
125 Inf. Helen Armstrong.
126 Parochial Church Council minute books held at Kirkoswald vicarage.
127 The author helped to organise these events.

benefices, and other chapels within the Methodist circuit, to be implemented after the retirement of Canon David Fowler in 2017.

Church Architecture

St Oswald's Church, Kirkoswald

Parts of the present building, the nave and chancel, and the north and south aisles, were dated to the 12th century by John Cory, the architect for the restoration in 1878/9, who described it as 'a small building c.1130, extended by pillars to support the roof, a new aisle c.1160 and a second aisle c.1180'.[128] A western extension of the nave, with chapels flanking the chancel, was added in the 14th century; and the chancel was rebuilt (and the chapels removed) in 1523, at which time a clerestory and a wooden north porch were added.[129] The size of the 1523 chancel, described in 1707 as 'much too large and too fine',[130] no doubt reflected Thomas, 2nd Lord Dacre's ambitions for his collegiate church. There was no tower attached to the church, but a bell tower with three bells stands on an adjacent hill: its existence is recorded in 1568, bellringers were paid wages in 1641,[131] and in 1814 the bell tower was painted white and described as 'a very conspicuous object'.[132] The present structure was raised in 1893.[133] The weather vane bears the date 1743.

The condition of the fabric of St Oswald's Church has many times caused anxiety through the centuries. In 1608 the chancel, windows, timber, walls and 'divers other places' were 'in great decay and the same ought to be repaired by the King's Majesty out of the tythes'.[134] The chancel was described in August 1673 as being 'in a ruinous condition and in imminent danger of a sudden fall',[135] and in 1681 as 'in total decay'.[136] By 1704/5 the roof had twice fallen in, and the impropriators Timothy Fetherstonhaugh and George Towry were presented for neglecting to repair it.[137] They seem to have done so by 1712, when the roof was 'large covered with lead'.[138] In 1814 the church roof was good.[139] In 1840 the Kirkoswald vestry resolved at a special meeting that 'in consideration of the uncomfortable state of the roof, ceiling and pews of the church a thorough repair be made': in December 1845 contractors were appointed and subscriptions of £300 were raised.[140] By 1847, 49 new pews had been installed on a new seating plan, all allocated

---

128 CAS (C), DX 835/3; for J.A. Cory, see Hyde & Pevsner, *Cumbria*, 62.
129 Hyde & Pevsner, *Cumbria*, 475.
130 Nicolson, *Misc. Acct.*, 115.
131 TNA, LR 2/213, field name Bellhouse Hill, 1568; CAS (C), PR 9/5, churchwardens' accounts 1641f; Fetherstonhaugh, B-10 for 1893 restoration.
132 *Diocese of Carlisle*, 243.
133 Fetherstonhaugh, B-10.
134 TNA, LR 2/212 (5 Apr. 1608, a survey of the rectory (*sic*) and tithes).
135 CAS (C), DSEN/14/3/1/102.
136 CAS (C), DRC 6/93 (1681).
137 Nicolson, *Misc. Act.*, 116, CAS (C), DRC 6/93 (1705).
138 CAS (C), DX 1915/3.
139 *Diocese of Carlisle*, 154.
140 CAS (C), PR 9/34.

to named families or properties.[141] In 1862 the interior of the church was said to be in excellent condition.[142] Nevertheless, further restoration to the ceilings of the nave and aisles, with the creation of a vestry and the installation of heating, was carried out between 1878 and 1879 under the direction of John Cory at a cost of about £1,400, all of which was raised by public subscription.[143] Hot-water pipes were installed in the church in 1884 and electric lighting in 1938–9.[144]

All Saints Church, Renwick

The church of All Saints, Renwick, of 1846, consists of a Norman-styled nave and chancel in grey stone, banded and decorated with red sandstone, located on a much older site to the north east of the village.[145] It is thought there may have been many earlier structures on this site, but no rebuilding was recorded before that of 1846. In 1704 the church was in a poor state of repair, 'without plaister, floor or glass'.[146] The owners of the tithes, William Towry of Croglin Hall and Philip Walker of Lazonby, were presented in 1704/5 for non-repair of the chancel, and Thomas Sowerby, who owned the glebe land, was said to be responsible for the repair of the quire; perhaps the responsibility was shared.[147] In 1747, Chancellor John Waugh of Carlisle noted that the Renwick parishioners had funded a 'clean new built little church' – thought to have been raised after James Westmorland became patron in 1739.[148] The church built in c.1740 was said to be in a 'very indifferent state' by 1814;[149] and was described in 1840 as 'a plain building consisting of nave and chancel, with a bell gable and entrance at the western end'.[150] It was replaced in 1846 by the present building. The cost of reconstruction was just under £500, of which the patron William de Lancy Lawson gave £230, George Nicholson £65, Queen's College Oxford £50, the Society for Building Churches £40, the curate John Watson £37, and the remaining sum (almost £88) was raised from the rates and small donations.[151]

141 CAS (C), PR 9/47.
142 L. Butler (ed.), *The Church Notes of Sir Stephen Glynne for Cumbria* (1833–72), CWAAS, Extra Ser. XXXVI (Kendal, 2011), 83.
143 CAS (C), PR 9/33; Fetherstonhaugh, B-22-12 (funding) and PR 9/27.
144 Fetherstonhaugh, B-14-10 91884); CAS (C), DX 1274/4 (1939).
145 Hyde and Pevsner, *Cumbria*, 588.
146 Nicolson, *Misc Acct.*, 119.
147 CAS (C), DRC 6/122 (Bishop's Transcripts); Nicolson *Misc. Acct.*, 119.
148 CAS (C), DMH 10/3/5, p.89 (and see above, Advowson).
149 *Diocese of Carlisle.*
150 Jefferson, *Hist. & Antiq.*, 107.
151 CAS (C), PR/72/13, page of accounts inserted in Register of Burials, Renwick.

Manorial Government

In 1569, when a swainmote court (so styled because it included Lazonby in the forest of Inglewood) was held in the name of the duke of Norfolk on behalf of the 5th Baron Dacre, then a child, Kirkoswald was grouped with Glassonby and Lazonby, and the steward was the duke's appointee John Myddleton.[1] Court baron sessions were held for Kirkoswald alone between 1619 and 1634 in the name of the Crown lessee Thomas Bartram: they dealt with appointment of township officers (constables, apprisers, aletasters, frithmen, surveyors and affearers), admittances, small claims, amercements for

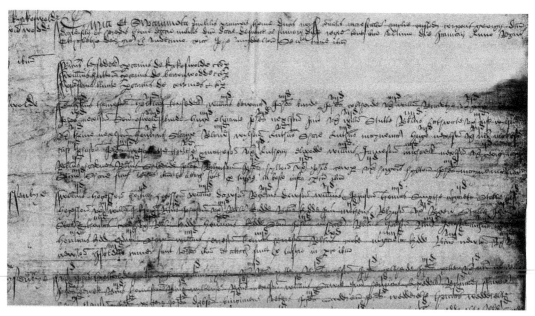

Figure 25 *The earliest surviving manor court roll (Arundel M517, 31 January 1569) for Kirkoswald and associated manors, held in the name of Thomas Howard 4th duke of Norfolk, guardian of the child George Lord Dacre, whose widowed mother the duke had married. Lord George died a few weeks later, and the manors passed in 1570 to the Crown on the attainder of the child's uncle Leonard Dacre.*

1   Arundel, M517.

husbandry offences and defamation, and administration of the market; and recorded the obligations of the tenantry to work boon days and deliver coal to Bartram.²

Staffield manor courts were held in the name of the king by the royal steward Henry Fetherstonhaugh from 1606 to his death in 1626, and his son Sir Timothy Fetherstonhaugh until 1642. In 1606, 1614 and 1624 various Staffield tenants were fined by manor courts for offences relating to pigs and livestock, upkeep of hedges and dykes, poaching fish in the Raven and slander and personal assault.³ In 1636 and 1639 the court appointed officers – appraisers, fencemen, houselookers and constables, and ordered that 'every ancient tenement within this lordship shall find a constable, and that the said office shall go from neighbour to neighbour according to ancient custom'. In addition to land administration and adjudicating small claims, the court imposed fines for unlawful removal of peat, offences related to animal husbandry, defective dykes, harbouring poachers and unauthorised cottagers, brewing ale without licence, common assault and slander, and bringing cases in other courts. Pains were made to allow any tenant to remove for their own use peat which had been cut and left at the site; for providing payment and refreshments for jurymen resolving boundary disputes; for requiring the making of satisfactory hedges and gates before 5 April in each year; for restraining the burning of heather on Whinfell; and for requiring the removal of animals from the common fields of Charbuckle Haresceugh between 15 April and the harvest.

After 1640 local government in both Kirkoswald and Staffield passed to the vestry, and when courts were resumed in the name of Francis Lennard – Staffield in 1650 and Kirkoswald in 1653 – business was largely confined to land administration and small claims. In Staffield, maintenance of hedges and dykes remained a priority, and in 1652, 1662, 1667 and 1670 hedge-lookers or frithmen were appointed separately for Croglin Water, Staffield, Scales and Blunderfield. A list of eight pains recorded in 1667 included graving of turves, ringing of swine, hedge and gate maintenance at Blunderfield and Raygarthfield, control of horses, removal of hurdles, removal of galls from the cornfields at Scarrowmanwick and unlawful use of dogs. In 1669 the tenantry resolved to share the cost of legal action to restrain unlawful use of, or encroachment upon, the commons. In 1670 several tenants were fined for not appearing when summoned by the bailiff to repair highways.

At Renwick, manor courts were held by stewards appointed by Queen's College.⁴ They included, for example, George Warwick, vicar of Great Salkeld (from 1609 to 1620); and John Bankes of Keswick (from 1624 to 1631), who was a lawyer who later rose to Attorney General of England and high judicial office under Charles I.⁵ Until 1600 the courts appointed village officers, but control over local administration seems to have passed to the vestry earlier than in Kirkoswald and Staffield.⁶ A particular problem for the College was a lack of confidence in the manor bailiff, paid 10s a year for collecting the rents and generally defending the rights of the manorial lords: in 1637 Thomas Lough, College fellow responsible for Renwick, writing to the newly appointed steward Lancelot

2   CAS (C), DMUS/1, box 8; Kirkoswald rolls survive for 1619, 1620, 1627, 1629/31, 1634; and fragments for 1637/40; the courts were styled Court Baron without Court Leat.
3   TNA, SC 2/165/17; LR 11/80/912; SC 2/165/22; CAS (C), DMUS/1/12/1.
4   QC, 5A series from 1561.
5   QC, 5A-48a, 5A-54; *ODNB*, Bankes, Sir John (1589–1644) (accessed 5 May 2017).
6   QC, 5A-47, copy made in 1656 of a 1597 court roll, now lost, in which a constable was appointed.

Dawes about the bailiff John Cowper, said 'Sir, you know him a crafty companion, & unles[s] you over-rule & make good inspection he will cheat us.'[7] The College sought, with mixed success, to retain their influence by appointing strong stewards like Bankes, or visitations like that of provost Langbaine in 1654, or through powerful Cumbrian allies like William Nicolson (later to become Bishop of Carlisle), who in 1691 dismissed the bailiff Thomas Gosling.[8] But in the long term, with the declining value of the rent roll (apart from coal mining which was controlled by lease), it ceased to be important to the College to retain control in Renwick.

In all three townships manorial tenancy administration was continued into the 20th century by law firms appointed to discharge the stewardship. Courts were occasionally held and juries appointed after 1900, but most business was conducted by the stewards in private. The last formal sitting of Renwick Manor Court was on 5 October 1925 at the reading room.[9]

Vestry Government[10]

In both Kirkoswald and Staffield local administration passed to the Kirkoswald vestry in 1640, and until 1708 township appointments were made in equal numbers, and accounts kept, for both Kirkoswald and Staffield. In 1708 the township of Staffield successfully applied to be allowed to administer their own poor relief and ceased to make appointments to Kirkoswald vestry.[11]

In each year the vestry appointed governors of the parish stock, churchwardens (except from 1668 to 1670), constables, overseers of the poor and assessors – two of each, one chosen from the Low Quarter, the other from the High Quarter. The two Kirkoswald governors of the parish stock were appointed from men who held either freehold or customary title to land, and between 1641 and 1660 the nominees were all farmers. The offices of churchwarden, constable and overseer rotated: in 1669 it was ordered by the parishioners that the office of churchwarden, left vacant in that year, should henceforth 'go according to the custom ... that every churchwarden appoint his next neighbour in course as formerly they have done'– implying that the house row system was in use in both Kirkoswald and Staffield.[12] After the split with Staffield in 1708, the governors were generally appointed from among men seen as offering experience and reliability, and from 1717 it was usual to reappoint from year to year. Jonathan Barnfather of Busk (d. 1773, farmer) held the office 16 times; Michael Nicholson of Townend (d. 1730, smallholder and tradesman) nine times; and eight other men for periods of three to five years. The other offices rotated: farmers still predominated, but the miller John Towlson

---

7   QC, 5A-63.
8   QC, 5A-89 and 171/2.
9   QC, Renwick court books.
10   CAS (C), PR 9/5 and PR9/34 and 35; after 1708 these records apply only to Kirkoswald, and there are no similar records for Renwick, nor for Staffield after 1708.
11   CAS (C), Q/6/1, p.512; above Soc. Hist. for the Bowman case 1693–1711.
12   As noted above in Relig. Hist., men were declining to serve as churchwarden during the years of conflict with the Independents.

Figure 26
*The first page (1641)
of the Kirkoswald
Churchwardens'
Account Book: in the
margin is written
'Love God and keep
his commandments';
note the entries
concerning Thomas
Browne of Keabourgh
and Anthony Browne
of Hyllend, both in
Staffield, which until
1708 was governed
by Kirkoswald vestry.
(Source: CAS (C), PR
9/5).*

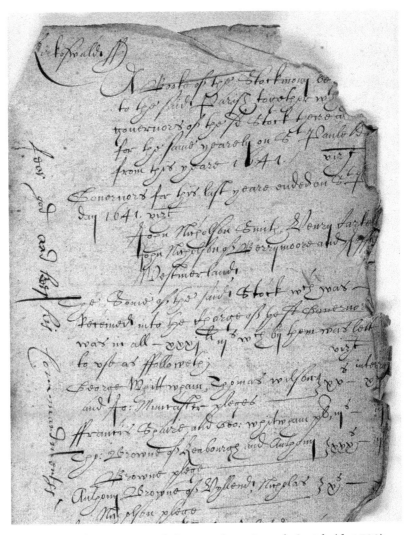

(d. 1725) served as churchwarden five times, and the merchant Joseph Smith (d. 1723) served as assessor nine times.[13]

By 1715 it was the practice of the overseers to present annual accounts, and by 1724 the churchwardens and constables were also doing so. Surveyors of highways were also recorded from 1696 to 1708. After 1740 the overseers and constables, who were responsible for collecting the land tax until 1760 (after which collectors of land tax were appointed), accounted separately for Low and High Quarters. The vestry concerned themselves occasionally with details of poor relief, recording two recipients of weekly pensions in 1707, and from 1745 lists of pensioners. They supervised the investment of the poor and school stocks and the application of interest. In 1753 they built a poorhouse in Kirkoswald, apparently disused by 1763.[14] The vestry dealt with the repair of the churchyard wall and the maintenance of the pinfold.

13   CAS (C), PR 9/5 for 1708–55; and see also manor court rolls for the same period.
14   Above Soc. Hist. also Fetherstonhaugh, *Our Cumberland Village*, 158, where a schedule of the goods belonging to the poorhouse of Kirkoswald is transcribed from a document, now lost, said to be dated 1775.

In 1791 an agreement was made with Sir Philip Musgrave for the use of a spring called Higher Common Well to supply water to Kirkoswald village. The supply was taken to the Townhead pump, the middle pump and the Market Cross pump, with extensions to the College and an inn.[15] After the creation of the Penrith Poor Law Union in 1836, the vestry met less frequently but continued to be active in other areas of parish governance, both civil and religious. They continued to appoint township officials (including from 1837 a surveyor of highways); and they revised the valuation list in 1838 and 1859–60. In 1842 they resolved to macadamise the village street.

In 1873 the recently appointed Penrith Rural Sanitary Committee received reports from their Medical Officer Dr J.D. Robertson about outbreaks of typhoid in Kirkoswald and Renwick, thought to be due to inadequate drainage. Kirkoswald was constituted a Special Drainage District and, following an inquiry in 1874, a scheme was prepared to be funded by a local rate. In 1875 the vestry commissioned drainage works and authorised the raising of funds, and by November of that year a new sewer (together with a parallel sewer in Back Lane) had been installed to drain into the Raven Beck.[16] This system was replaced in 1967 with a sewage works at Lowfield.[17] A scheme for drainage works and the removal of nuisances was also approved for Renwick and – after delays caused by Joseph Nicholson of Ravenwood – completed in 1879.

Improved sewerage was not enough to free these townships from the threat of water-borne disease and in 1888, after a public inquiry, a system of piped water was installed in Renwick.[18] Likewise in Kirkoswald, the vestry considered, from 1887, several schemes for improving the water supply to the whole village, and in 1892 agreed to new water works with tanks and an iron pipe, using the same source of supply, the cost to be defrayed by a water charge upon the consumers. The scheme also included carrying the water main down the back street from Townhead. By 1894 these works had been completed.[19]

A police officer was stationed in Kirkoswald by 1854: a police house was provided in 1925 in Sandhill, and replaced in 1960. In 1990 the house was sold and there was no longer a resident police officer in the village.[20]

Post-1894 Arrangements

The Penrith Rural District Council came into being in 1895, and in the same year were constituted Kirkoswald parish council, Staffield parish meeting and Renwick parish meeting.[21] In Kirkoswald early consideration was given to street lighting, and a motion to adopt the Lighting & Watch Act 1833 and to light the township with oil lamps was defeated in 1895. Electric street lighting was eventually installed in 1933 and Kirkoswald

15 *Mid Cumberland and North Westmorland Herald*, 22 Dec. 1891 and 14 Jan. 1896.
16 CAS (C), SRDP/1/1/1, pp. 29, 38, 84.
17 CAS (C), SRDP/1/3/30.
18 CAS (C), SRDP/1/1, pp. 13/18, 63, 100, 176; SRDP/3/4/4; *Penrith Observer*, 3 Jan. and 29 May 1888.
19 CAS (C), PR 9/35; OS Map, 1:2500 Cumb., Sheet XL-6 (1900 edn) records a covered reservoir on the Higher Common.
20 Inf. Neville Jackson and John Haugh; a policeman called Jonas Catherall is recorded at CAS (C), Q/PL/4, 38 (1854); a resident constable was enumerated in the 1861 census (Kirkoswald household 84).
21 CAS (C), SPC/117/1/1 (Kirkoswald); CAS (C), SPC/17/1 (Staffield); SPC/35/1/1 (Renwick).

Figure 27 *Kirkoswald war memorial, market square, with the Old Post Office on the left, the Fetherston Arms on the right and High College beyond.*

was connected to the national grid in January 1934.[22] There was occasional expenditure on repair of footbridges, and after 1910 small sums were contributed to heating and lighting the Church Institute.[23] In 1912 the village water supply (still obtained from Higher Common) was extended to Town End.[24] In 1928 it was planned to take a new supply from the mill dam on Cannerheugh Gill to serve Busk and Parkhead, with an onward connection via Highbankhill to the reservoir on Higher Common; but implementation of this was delayed and Parkhead did not receive a mains water supply until after 1945.[25]

In Staffield in 1898 the parish meeting appointed an assistant overseer at £11 p.a. (continued in each year to 1920); and in 1903 a manager of Kirkoswald school. Concern for

22   CAS (C), SPC/117/1/2 (1933); *Cumberland and Westmorland Herald*, 13 Jan. 1934.
23   CAS (C), SPC/117/2/1.
24   *Mid Cumberland and North Westmorland Herald*, 11 Feb. 1896, 17 Feb. 1912.
25   CAS (C), SRDP/3/4/22, a 1928 map showing the proposed scheme; inf. John Haugh.

Figure 28 *A view taken from Hartside Fell towards the north-west and the Solway Firth; the building on the right is Outhwaite Farm, Renwick; the Raven Beck (hidden) flows east to west this side of the farmhouse; the rising ground in the middle distance (left of centre) is the former Whinfell Common, Staffield, and the River Eden (hidden) flows south to north beyond that; on a clear day the waters of the Firth and the hills of Galloway, Scotland, can be seen.*

roads and bridges was the most frequently raised issue: in 1899 the parish meeting rejected a proposal to upgrade the road to Staffield Hall and Fieldgarth farms; and the need for a bridge over Croglin Water at Dale was discussed (and a subscription was authorised, but not it seems acted upon). In 1915 general concern was recorded about the poor condition of roads in Staffield. The parish meeting in Renwick also appointed school managers, and (in 1912) trustees of the Percival Charity. They also concerned themselves with the management of the reading room until, after an inquiry by the Charity Commissioners in 1913, it was established that the building belonged to Queen's College.[26]

In 1934 Kirkoswald civil parish was enlarged to include Staffield and Renwick.[27] From 1934 to 2016 the parish council continued to meet monthly, raising a precept (mainly applied to grants to support community organisations), administering small parcels of parish council land (registered in the 1990s)[28] and responding to planning applications. In addition the council has given encouragement to community enterprise such as entry into 'Best Kept Village' competitions (which Kirkoswald won in 1958 to 1960, 1963, 1971, 1974 and 1978), and the research and writing of this volume.[29]

26   CAS (C), PR/72/7.
27   Cumberland Review Order 1934.
28   CAS (C), Q/RE/125, Kirkoswald enclosure 1876, plot 76 (Berrimoor Common).
29   'Best Kept Village' victory records held at the Church Institute.

ABBREVIATIONS

The following abbreviations and short titles have been used.

Arundel	Muniments of the Duke of Norfolk, Arundel Castle
CAS (C)	Cumbria Archive Service (Carlisle)
Book of Fees	*The Book of Fees* (3 vols, HMSO, 1920–31)
Calamy Revised, ed. A.G. Matthews	Calamy Revised: Being a Revision of Edmund Calamy's *Account of the Ministers and Others Ejected and Silenced*, 1660–2, ed. A.G. Matthews (Oxford, 1934)
Cal. Bord. Pap.	*Calendar of Border Papers preserved in the Public Record Office* (HMSO, 1894)
Cal. Cttee for Compounding	*Calendar of the Proceedings of the Committee for Compounding with Delinquents*, etc. (HMSO, 1889–92)
Cal. Fine	*Calendar of Fine Rolls preserved in the Public Record Office* (HMSO, 1911–62)
Cal. Inq. Misc.	*Calendar of Inquisitions preserved in the Public Record Office* (HMSO, 1916–68)
Cal. Pat.	*Calendar of the Patent Rolls preserved in the Public Record Office* (HMSO, 1891–1986)
Census	Census Report (printed)
Cockermouth	*Cockermouth Congregational Church Book (1651–c.1765)*, ed. R.B. Wordsworth (CWAAS Record Ser. XXI, 2012).
CWAAS	*Cumberland & Westmorland Antiquarian & Archaeological Society*
Denton's History	*John Denton's History of Cumberland*, ed. A.J.L. Winchester, Surtees Society vol. 213 and CWAAS Record Ser. vol. XX (Woodbridge, 2010)

Denton, *Perambulation*	*Thomas Denton: a perambulation of Cumberland 1687–1688, including descriptions of Westmorland, The Isle of Man and Ireland,* ed. A.J.L. Winchester with Mary Wane, Surtees Society vol. 207 and CWAAS Record Ser. vol. XVI (Woodbridge, 2003)
Diocese of Carlisle	*The Diocese of Carlisle, 1814–1855: Chancellor Walter Fletcher's 'Diocesan Book', with additional material from Bishop Percy's parish notebooks,* ed. J. Platt, Surtees Society vol. 219 and CWAAS Record Ser. vol. XXII (Woodbridge, 2015)
Dir. Cumb.	*Directory of Cumberland*
Dir. C&W	*Directory of Cumberland and Westmorland*
Eden, *State of the Poor*	Sir Frederick Morton Eden, *The State of the Poor* (1797)
Educ. Enq. Abstract	*Education Enquiry Abstract for 1833* (Parliamentary Papers 1835 (62), xii)
Educ. of Poor Digest	*Digest of Returns to the Select Committee on Education of the Poor in 1818* (Parliamentary Papers 1819 (224), ix (1))
ERO	Essex Record Office, Chelmsford
Fetherstonhaugh	Muniments of the Fetherstonhaugh family of the College, Kirkoswald
Fetherstonhaugh, *Our Cumberland Village*	Col. Timothy Fetherstonhaugh, *Our Cumberland Village* (1925)
Graham, 'Arthuret, Kirklinton and Kirkoswald'	T.H.B. Graham, 'Arthuret, Kirklinton and Kirkoswald', *CW2*, XXVIII (1928), 41–58
Heysham's Census	Dr Heysham's Census of the Diocese of Carlisle, 1781, Carlisle Central Library, Jackson Collection, M839
HMSO	Her Majesty's Stationery Office
Hutchinson, *Hist. Cumb.*	William Hutchinson, *History of the County of Cumberland and some places adjacent,* (2 vols, Carlisle, 1794)
Hyde & Pevsner, *Cumbria*	M. Hyde and N. Pevsner, *Cumbria: Cumberland, Westmorland and Furness.* The Buildings of England (2010)
Jefferson, *Hist. & Antiq.*	S. Jefferson, *The History and Antiquities of Leath Ward, in the County of Cumberland: with biographical notices and memoirs* (Carlisle, 1840)

Lanercost Cart.	*The Lanercost Cartulary*, ed. J.M. Todd (Surtees Society, vol. 203, 1997)
L. & P. Hen. VIII	*Letters and Papers, Foreign and Domestic, of the Reign of Henry VIII* (HMSO, 1864–1932)
Lysons, *Magna Britannia: Cumb.*	Daniel Lysons and Samuel Lysons, *Magna Britannia: Volume 4, Cumberland* (1816)
Nicolson, *Misc. Acct.*	William Nicolson, *Miscellany Accounts of the Diocese of Carlisle*, ed. R.S. Ferguson (Carlisle, 1877)
N&B	Joseph Nicolson and Richard Burn, *The History and Antiquities of the Counties of Westmorland and Cumberland*, 2 vols (1777; facsimile reprint, Wakefield, 1976)
Nightingale, *Ejected of 1662*	B. Nightingale, *The Ejected of 1662 in Cumberland and Westmorland* (2 vols, Manchester, 1911)
NHLE	The National Heritage List for England
ODNB	*Oxford Dictionary of National Biography*
OS	Ordnance Survey
Pedigrees Visitations	*Pedigrees recorded at the heralds' visitations of the counties of Cumberland and Westmorland: made by Richard St. George, Norry, king of arms in 1615, and by William Dugdale, Norry, king of arms in 1666*, ed. J. Foster (Carlisle and Kendal, 1891)
Perriam and Robinson, *Medieval Fortified Buildings*	Denis R. Perriam and John Robinson, *The Medieval Fortified Buildings of Cumbria: an illustrated gazetteer and research guide* (CWAAS Extra Ser. XXIX, 1998)
Poor Law Com. 1st Rep.	*First Report of the Poor Law Commission* (Parliamentary Papers 1835 (44), Appendix (B.1), Answers to the Rural Queries)
PNC	A.M. Armstrong, A. Mawer, F.M. Stenton and Bruce Dickins, *The Place-Names of Cumberland*, English Place-Name Society (3 vols, Cambridge, 1950–2)
Priory of Hexham	*The Black Book of the Priory of Hexham*, ed. J. Raine (2 vols, Surtees Society, vol. 46, 1865)
QC	Muniments of The Queen's College Oxford
RCHM	Royal Commission on Historical Monuments
Reg. John de Halton	*The Register of John de Halton, Bishop of Carlisle A.D. 1292–1324*, eds. W.N. Thompson & T.F. Tout, 2 vols, Cant. & York Soc., 12–13 (1913).

Reg. John Kirkby	*The Register of John Kirkby, Bishop of Carlisle A.D. 1325–32*, ed. R.L. Storey, 2 vols, Cant. & York Soc., 79 & 81 (Woodbridge, 1993–95)
Reg. Wetheral	*The Register of the Priory of Wetherhal*, ed. J.E. Prescott (London & Kendal, 1897)
5th Rep. Com. Char.	5th Report of the Commissioners Appointed to Enquire Concerning *Charities* (Parliamentary Papers 1821 (159) xii)
Rot. Chart.	*Rotuli Chartarum, 1199–1216*, ed. T. D. Hardy (Record Commission, 1837)
Rot. Lit.	*Rotuli Litterarum Patentium in Turri Londinensi Asservati*, ed. T. D. Hardy (Record Commission, 1835)
Tax. Eccl.	*Taxatio Eccliastica Angliae et Walliae auctoritate P. Nicholai IV circa A.D. 1291*, ed. S. Ayscough and J. Caley (Rec. Com., 1802)
Thompson, 'Dean Barwick'	B.L. Thompson, 'Dean Barwick and his Will', *CW2*, LXV (1965), 240f.
Tiffin, 'Memories of Kirkoswald'	Maurice John Tiffin, 'Memories of Kirkoswald' (*c.*1970)
TNA	The National Archives, Kew
Val. Eccl.	*Valor Ecclesiasticus temp. Hen. VIII auctoritate regia Institutus*, ed. J. Caley and J. Hunter (6 vols, Rec. Com., 1810–34)

Manuscript Sources

This note discusses the main manuscript sources used in writing the history of Kirkoswald and Renwick. It is not comprehensive and should be used in conjunction with the List of Abbreviations.

Public Repositories

Cumbria Archive Service, Carlisle holds material relating to the part of the historic county of Cumberland north of the River Derwent. Records held there include those of Church of England Parishes, Nonconformist Churches, Local Authorities, and the Diocese of Carlisle, as well as collections of family and estate papers.

DB 74	Clark, Scott-Harden estate agents of Penrith
DFCCL 13	Lancashire Congregational Union: Cumberland District
DFCM 4	Kirkoswald Methodist Circuit
DMUS	Musgrave family of Eden Hall, Edenhall
DRC 5	Diocese of Carlisle, Visitation; Correction Court, 1663–1932
DSEN	Senhouse family of Netherhall, Maryport
DVAN	Fletcher Vane family, Lords Inglewood of Hutton, Hutton-in-the-Forest
PR 9	Records of St Oswald Parish, Kirkoswald
PROB	Diocese of Carlisle probate records, 1548–1858
Q	Cumberland Quarter Sessions, 1668–1948
SRDP	Penrith Rural District Council: Minute books of Rural Sanitary Authority/ council and committees 1872–1973; Rate books 1927–1974; Valuation lists 1929–1973; Building control plans 1898–1974

Essex Record Office, Chelmsford holds the Barrett-Lennard Collection. The Lennard family, Lords Dacre of the South, owned a group of manors in Cumberland and Westmorland from 1649 to 1716: the papers held at Chelmsford explain how they came to acquire them, and also much of interest to Cumbrian historians during those years.

The National Archives at Kew, London, holds the records of national government from the late 12th century onwards. The principal documents used in this history include:

C 132–136	Records of the court of Chancery, Inquisitions post mortem
E 134	Exchequer, King's Remembrancer, Depositions taken by Commission
E 178	Exchequer, King's Remembrancer, Special Commissions of Inquiry
E 179	Exchequer, King's Remembrancer: Particulars of Account and other records relating to Lay and Clerical Taxation
HO 129	Home Office, Ecclesiastical Census Returns, 1851
LR	Office of the Auditors of Land Revenue and predecessors, Miscellaneous Books
MAF 32	Ministry of Food, National Farm Survey, Individual Farm Records, 1941–1943
RG 4	General Register Office, Registers of Births, Marriages and Deaths surrendered to the Non-parochial Registers Commissions of 1837 and 1857
SC 2	Special Collections, Court Rolls
SC 11	Special Collections, Rentals and Surveys, Rolls

Private Collections

Muniments of the Queen's College Oxford, 5A series, relating to Renwick manor.

Muniments of the Fetherstonhaugh family of the College, Kirkoswald are retained by Timothy Fetherstonhaugh at the College, Kirkoswald, and can be seen upon application to him there.

Records relating to the Dacre family estates are also held among the **Muniments of the Duke of Norfolk, Arundel Castle** ['Arundel' in Abbreviations]. Of particular help was Helen Warne, *The Duke of Norfolk's Deeds at Arundel Castle the Dacre Estates in Northern Counties* (Chichester, 2006).

Printed Sources

Primary Sources

The most important printed primary sources, including calendars of major classes in The National Archives, are included in the List of Abbreviations. Among the most useful have been the *Calendar of the Patent Rolls* and the *Calendar of Border Papers*.

The Cumberland & Westmorland Antiquarian & Archaeological Society (CWAAS) and Surtees Society have jointly published a number of transcribed sources. Three of these publications have been used widely in this study, namely, *John Denton's History of Cumberland*; *Thomas Denton: a perambulation of Cumberland 1687–1688, including descriptions of Westmorland, The Isle of Man and Ireland*; and *The Diocese of Carlisle, 1814–1855: Chancellor Walter Fletcher's 'Diocesan Book', with additional material from Bishop Percy's parish notebooks.*

A large number of trade directories are cited in this book, including those published by Bulmer, Kelly, Parson & White, Mannix & Whellan and the Post Office. An abbreviated version of the title (usually *Dir. Cumb.* or *Dir. C&W*) has been used, given together with the publisher and dates.

Books

Several antiquarian texts specific to the history of Cumbria have been used where the information given appears to derive from a contemporary primary source. These include S. Jefferson's *The History and Antiquities of Leath Ward, in County of Cumberland* (Carlisle, 1840) and Daniel and Samuel Lysons, *Magna Britannia: Volume 4, Cumberland* (London, 1816).

Invaluable to this study have been various articles published in Cumberland & Westmorland Antiquarian & Archaeological Society (CWAAS) *Transactions*, the series of which are abbreviated as follows:

CW1   *Transactions of the CWAAS*, old series (1866–1900)

CW2   *Transactions of the CWAAS*, new series (1901–2000)

CW3   *Transactions of the CWAAS*, third series (2001–)

One of the most frequently used articles within this research is T.H.B. Graham, 'Arthuret, Kirklinton and Kirkoswald', *CW2*, XXVIII (1928), 41–58.

Some elements of Kirkoswald's history that are unrecorded elsewhere have been illuminated by two key local publications, namely, Colonel Timothy Fetherstonhaugh's *Our Cumberland Village*, privately published in 1925 (relied upon where the author writes from his own knowledge) and 'Memories of Kirkoswald'. The latter is an eight-page manuscript, unsigned and undated: it is believed (from internal evidence) to have been written in about 1970 by Maurice John Tiffin (1897–1977), who was born (and died) in Kirkoswald. The text can be examined on the Kirkoswald page of the CCHT website: www.cumbriacountyhistory.org.uk.

The main source for architectural history is M. Hyde and N. Pevsner, *The Buildings of England: Cumbria* (2010).

Websites

Anglo American Legal Tradition, http://aalt.law.uh.edu.

Historic England's Red Box Collection, https://historicengland.org.uk/images-books/
        photos/englands-places.

National Heritage List for England, https://historicengland.org.uk/listing/the-list/.

Oxford Dictionary of National Biography, http://www.oxforddnb.com/.

advowson: the patronage of a church (see 'patron' below).

agistment: taking in cattle from outside the manor to store and feed on commons.

amercement: a fine imposed by the manor court.

assart: to clear waste or common ground for arable or pasture.

attainder: being found guilty of treason.

bailiff: the tenant appointed by the lord of the manor to collect the rent.

barytes: sulphate of barium or heavy spar, a chemical ingredient.

bay: in architecture, a unit of a building regularly divided from the next by features such as columns or windows.

boon service: an unpaid service due by a tenant to the lord of the manor.

boot: (regional) the tenants' allowance of timber from the lord's woodland, for use in buildings, furnishings and farm implements (domestic fires burned peat).

bovate: as much land as one ox could plough in a ploughing season (15 to 20 a.)

cattlegate: an allowance of pasture for a specified number of beasts.

common: undivided land held in joint occupation by a community (see 'common fields', 'waste').

common lodging house: a house, other than an inn, in which lodgings were let.

common (open) fields: communal agrarian organisation under which an individual's farmland was held in scattered strips (dales, q.v.) adjoining similar strips owned by other farmers.

constablewick: a township appointing its own constable(s), whose duties would include levying and collecting local taxation.

customary tenure: unfree tenure regulated by local manorial custom – including rent which, if customary, remained unchanged in perpetuity.

dale: (regional) a strip of land within an undivided (common) field.

demesne: in the Middle Ages, land held by a lord of the manor, rather than granted to tenants; later, usually leased to farmers for terms of years.

dispark: to enclose land within a park (q.v.) for agricultural use.

dissent (-ing, -er): to differ from the doctrine of the Church of England, usually joining other religious groupings for worship.

enclosure: the process by which open fields and commons were divided into fields for exclusive use, either by voluntary agreement or statutory procedure.

enfeoff: (medieval) to invest another person with the freehold of lands.

enfranchisement: the conversion of customary tenancies into freehold.

entry fine: a payment due to the lord of the manor by a tenant taking possession of a customary tenement (see also 'general demission').

fulling (mill): the process of cleansing and thickening cloth by beating and washing.

frithmen: (regional) men appointed by the community to oversee use of the commons

garth: (regional) a small piece of enclosed ground adjoining a farmstead.

general demission: the simultaneous termination of all customary tenancies in a manor (e.g. on death of the lord of the manor, or a collective act of treason)

glebe: land assigned to the clergyman of a church for his support and the endowment of the church.

greenhew: the right to cut greenery for fodder, and the payment for that right.

hearth tax: royal tax imposed in the 1660s, assessed on the number of hearths or fireplaces in each taxpayer's house.

impropriator: a lay person who has acquired the title to former glebe land and/or to collect tithes for personal use.

intake: a piecemeal enclosure from the common, with or without permission.

manor: an area of landed property, with tenants regulated by a court held in the name of the lord of the manor: a **chief lord** (if not the monarch) held from the Crown; a **mesne lord** held from the chief lord; either might hold courts.

messuage: portion of land, generally with a house and outbuildings on it.

modus: a money payment in lieu of tithe (q.v.).

moiety: one of two (or more) parts into which a manor or parcel of land is divided.

nonconformity: refusal to conform to the doctrine and discipline of the Church of England.

overseer: an officer appointed annually by vestry (q.v.) to administer poor relief.

pain: (regional) a regulation made by a manor court.

pannage: pasturage (e.g. beechnuts) for pigs.

patron (of a church): the person having the right to nominate a candidate to the bishop for appointment as incumbent clergyman of a church.

park: an enclosed tract of land held by royal grant or prescription for keeping beasts of the chase (usually deer).

peel tower: a small fortified building, common in an area vulnerable to Scottish raiding.

perpetual curate: a clergyman appointed to a parish church by its patron.

poorhouse: a house provided to accommodate persons in receipt of poor relief.

poor stock: a fund held by parish officers, mainly accumulated from bequests in wills, and applied to (among other purposes) the relief of the poor.

presentment: a formal complaint to higher authority of some offence or default.

Protestation Return: the list returned by each parish in March 1642 of all men aged 18 and over who had made a solemn affirmation of loyalty to Crown and Parliament.

purvey: (Cumberland) a land tax collected in each constablewick towards public expenditure by county and parish officials (replaced by rates in 1791).

shambles: a place where meat is sold.

statesman: (regional) a freeholder or customary tenant who works his own land.

styca: low value, copper-alloy coin.

stint: the number of animals a tenant was allowed to graze on the common pasture.

tenant right: (regional) a form of customary tenure, thought to be related to a military service obligation, allowing automatic inheritance on the death of a tenant.

tenement: a farmhold held from the lord of the manor, normally, in 17th-century Cumberland, 30–40 a.

tithes: the tenth part of the agricultural produce paid (originally) to the parish clergyman.

township: (regional meaning) a local division of a large parish (or the whole of a small parish), containing a village, (usually) an administrative unit for local taxation.

vernacular: (architectural) building design typically used in a locality.

vestry: assembly of leading parishioners, responsible for poor relief and parish administration before 1895.

waste: uncultivated land.

yeoman: a man of respectable standing in his community usually owning and cultivating a small freehold or customary estate.

INDEX

CPSIA information can be obtained
at www.ICGtesting.com
Printed in the USA
JSHW062301080223
37476JS00004B/32

9 781912 702046